Sydney

Front cover and
right: aspects
of the Sydney
Opera House

Sydney's glorious harbour · Venture out onto the water to explore the harbour's many facets by ferry, yacht or cruiser *(page 26)*

Sydney Harbour Bridge ·
More than just a transport link –
an elegant work of art in
grey steel *(page 34)*

Art Gallery of New South Wales · An impressive showcase of international, Aboriginal and modern Australian art *(page 40)*

Sydney Aquarium · Whe the Great Barrier Reef comes to the city *(page 5.*

Sydney Opera House With its wondrous billowing sails and prominent setting on the harbour, it's an architectural triumph and the city's pride and joy *(page 36)*

Taronga Zoo Among the inmates are koalas and kangaroos *(page 28)*

Royal Botanic Gardens Lush and peaceful, with great harbour views *(page 38)*

Blue Mountains Wilderness on the city's doorstep *(page 73)*

The Rocks The maritime-flavoured, historic heart of Sydney *(page 30)*

Bondi Beach A short distance from the city centre is Sydney's favourite ocean playground *(page 66)*

CONTENTS

41

99

69

82

103

94

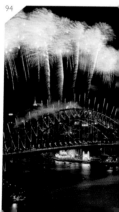

Features

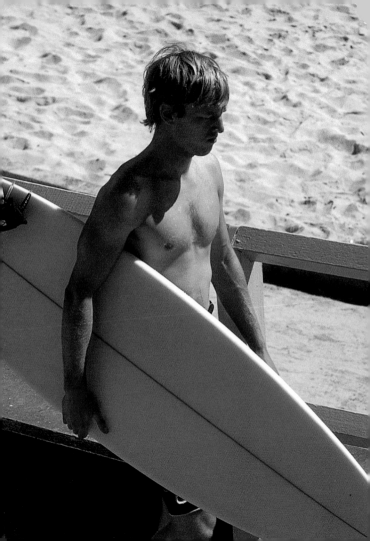

INTRODUCTION

Sunny, surf-fringed Sydney – gateway to the country for many visitors to Australia – seems custom-built for outdoor enjoyment. Bold, bright and alluring, the city glows with instant sensuous appeal. Airline passengers approaching Sydney International Airport at dawn (the time when many international flights touch down) may enjoy views of mists lifting slowly from the grey-green, eucalyptus-filled valleys on Sydney's outskirts. These richly forested landscapes then give way to terracotta roofs and glittering swimming pools as Australia's biggest and most cosmopolitan city emerges. If you fly in later in the day, the lights from the city skyline, as well as from Sydney's beaches and the yachts bobbing in its harbour, are displayed to full advantage.

The city's glorious harbour, stretching about 20km (12½ miles) inland from the Pacific Ocean to the east, is its dominant feature, and was what induced the commanders of the first convict fleet to make their settlement here. The city is now a sprawling metropolis extending more than 40km (25 miles) west, 20km (12 miles) south and 15km (9 miles) north of the harbour. The urban area is surrounded on all sides by vast national parks, most notably the Blue Mountains National Park to the west, so the city's inhabitants are never far from pristine bush wilderness.

Just over 4 million people, a fifth of Australia's population, choose to live here and Sydney is regularly ranked as one of the world's favourite tourist destinations. It's easy to see why – if the world had a lifestyle capital, Sydney would be a strong contender. The city seamlessly combines all the advantages of big-city living – a vibrant arts and leisure scene,

Sydney's ocean-facing beaches attract the surf crowd

'green bans', where members refused to carry out any destructive work. Similarly, the overwhelming success of the 2000 Olympics was largely down to the enthusiasm and drive of the city's people.

The cultural and ethnic mix of that population is constantly evolving thanks to successive waves of immigration. The influence of the original British immigrants is still very much in evidence. Students at some of Sydney's private schools wear blazers and straw boaters just like their counterparts in Britain, cricket is played on local greens and if you stroll past Sydney's Supreme Court in Macquarie Street, you can see lawyers in flowing black gowns and horsehair wigs, who would be at home in London's Inns of Court.

Many other ethnic influences are also at work. The opening up of Australia since the end of World War II to immigration from all sources has transformed Sydney to the point where a third of the city's population was born outside Australia. After English, the city's main languages are Chinese, Italian, Greek and Vietnamese. Australia as a whole has begun to embrace its geographical proximity to Asia: Chinese, Indonesian and Japanese are taught in many schools and China, Japan and Korea are among its most important trading partners.

From a society of meat-and-potato eaters and beer drinkers, Sydney has been transformed into a multicultural society with a Mediterranean and Asian flavour. Locals are often found sipping cappuccinos or white wine these days rather than knocking back glasses of beer, and Chinese, Thai and Vietnamese restaurants do a brisk trade throughout the city.

A BRIEF HISTORY

What Sydney's history lacks in length, it makes up for in colour. In two centuries of existence, the city has had more than its share of wild characters. They include tyrants such as Captain Bligh, notorious commander of the warship HMS *Bounty*, who survived a shipboard mutiny to find himself dispatched to Sydney as Governor of New South Wales.

A lesser-known figure was James Hardy Vaux, charming pickpocket and swindler, transported in chains from England to Australia three times – a record. Each time Vaux managed to return to England, they caught him and sent him back again.

Bennelong, the first Aborigine to learn English and wear clothes, was a more respectable individual. He travelled to London, where King George III (in one of his saner moods)

Aboriginal rockpainting in central New South Wales

gave him a coat. He returned to Sydney in 1795 and lived in a hut on the point where the Opera House now stands.

Dreamtime Echoes

Australia has been populated by modern humans for longer than Western Europe – possibly twice as long. Australia's original inhabitants are thought to have arrived between 40,000 and 60,000 years ago during the great Pleistocene Ice Age, crossing a land bridge from Southeast Asia. When Cook landed, the area around Sydney was inhabited by the Eora people, one of 600 or so Aboriginal tribes living in Australia. These tribes spoke many languages, some utterly dissimilar to one another. The word Eora, in the local Sydney-area language, simply meant 'here' or 'in this place'.

Aborigines lived within tribal boundaries they believed had been created by hero ancestors in a period called the Dreamtime. Dreamtime legends detail the significance of every tree, rock and river and explain how humans can live in harmony with nature; Aboriginal art expressed these and other spiritual beliefs. Trading paths and trails ran throughout Australia and were often invested with ceremonial or magical qualities. They connected waterholes, food sources and landmarks.

Aborigines built no permanent structures but lived in a way that ensured their survival in an often harsh environment. They foraged, fished and hunted kangaroo, wallaby, goanna lizards and other native beasts with spears and boomerangs. They ate berries, roots and insects such as the witchetty grub (a large white grub about the size of a finger) and the bogong moth; the latter two were roasted on open fires before consumption.

Aboriginal names

A number of locations in Sydney have Aboriginal names. Bondi means 'sound of rushing waters'; Coogee means 'rotten seaweed'; Ku-ring-gai is the name of the tribe that lived there; and Cronulla means 'small pink shells'.

A 1799 depiction of the founding of the colony

Colonists in Chains

In 1770 renowned English navigator Captain Cook spied the hills of eastern Australia and, reminded of the landscapes of southern Wales, coined the name New South Wales. He landed on Australia's east coast and explored Botany Bay, a short distance south of where Sydney now stands and today the site of Sydney Airport's third runway. Cook claimed all the territory he charted for King George III. While the Dutch (and possibly the Spanish, Portuguese and Chinese) had visited Australia before him, Cook's arrival was to have the greatest effect.

The British soon decided that Australia was an ideal place to send its convicts. In the late 18th century, Britain's prisons were at bursting point, and when the American War of Independence inconveniently interrupted the orderly transportation of convicts to America and the Caribbean (where they were used as virtual slave labour on plantations), the government decided Sydney would make the perfect penal colony. Britain at one stage had declared that 223 offences were punishable by death (including the crime of 'breaking down the head or mound of any fish-pond'); in practice, however, people were hanged for only 25 of these, leaving plenty of convicts to be transported to one of the farthest-flung corners of its Empire.

The first 'prisoner-colonists' arrived in 1788. Under the command of retired naval officer Captain Arthur Phillip, the First Fleet consisted of eleven vessels carrying 1,030 people, including 548 male and 188 female convicts. The convicts were repeat offenders; their crimes usually involved theft. None was a murderer though – for that, you were hanged.

After briefly visiting Botany Bay, Phillip anchored in Port Jackson (named but not visited by Cook) to the north, which he described as 'the finest harbour in the world'. The fleet sailed into the semi-circular bay now known as Circular Quay. This they named Sydney Cove, after Thomas Townshend, Viscount Sydney, the secretary of state for the colonies.

The Eora on the shore showed no fear of the light-skinned foreigners and their ships. But they were curious. A British officer, Captain Watkin Tench, describes how an Aboriginal man closely examined a white child's skin, hat and clothes, 'muttering to himself all the while'. Despite such friendly encounters, the British saw the Aborigines as uncivilised nomads and took possession of their lands without treaty or compensation.

Irish influx

The transportation of convicts from Britain helped make Australia the most Irish country outside Ireland. After British troops crushed the Irish rebellion of 1798, thousands of suspected rebels were hanged, tortured, or transported. In 1800, almost all white Australians were English by birth or ancestry. Just eight years later, more than 20 percent were Irish.

In the first few months of its existence, the fledgling colony of petty thieves, sailors and soldiers ran headlong into famine. Starvation threatened, but Britain continued to send new shiploads of colonists. It was not until the foundation of an agricultural colony in Parramatta (25km/15½ miles to the west) in 1790 that the threat of starvation receded.

Back in Britain the Home Secretary, Lord Bathurst (a Sydney street is named after him), declared he wanted criminals to regard the threat of transportation to Australia as 'an object of real terror'. It was made clear to all that colonial Governor Phillip was authorised to summarily jail, flog or hang anyone in New South Wales. Britain sent a Second Fleet to Sydney in 1790 – then a third. Merciless floggings with the cat-o'-nine-tails (generally administered about 40 lashes a time, but sometimes over 100) kept a semblance of order – even if the punishment sometimes killed the recipients.

Rum hospital

The construction of Sydney's first hospital on Macquarie Street in 1812 was financed by giving the builders a monopoly of the rum trade. One wing is now Parliament House, another is the Mint; Sydney Hospital stands on the site of the long-demolished middle wing.

Rum Legacy

Relations with the Eora and other Aboriginal tribes soured as rum and diseases introduced from the west took their toll. By 1840 the tribal life of Sydney's Aborigines had been destroyed. Sydney's Aboriginal population dwindled to just a few hundred by the end of the

19th century, as many Aborigines fled their traditional lands. Today, less than 1 percent of the city's population is Aboriginal.

When Governor Phillip retired, the military took over. The colony's top army officer, Major Francis Grose, cornered the rum market. His troops, nicknamed the Rum Corps, made fortunes in liquor racketeering. Sydney became one of the hardest-drinking settlements in the world, addicted to fiery Brazilian *aguardiente* and cheap spirits distilled in Bengal. Tradesmen were frequently paid in rum.

Captain Bligh

London eventually sent out a harsh disciplinarian to shake up the rum-sodden militia. Captain William Bligh was famous well before his arrival, having been set adrift in a longboat after the notorious mutiny on the warship HMS *Bounty* in 1789. Rather than perish at sea as the mutineers had expected, Bligh and his 18 companions had sailed from Tahiti to Timor, a journey of about 6,400km (4,000 miles), one of the longest voyages ever accomplished in an open boat. When Bligh was appointed Governor of New South Wales in 1805, his legendary temper soon earned him the nickname Caligula, after one of the most hated and feared Roman emperors.

On 26 January 1808, as Bligh was toasting the 20th anniversary of Sydney's founding, a group of his officers

Hyde Park Barracks, designed by Francis Greenway

mutinied and took him prisoner. The Rum Rebellion, as the uprising became known, deposed Bligh and held him under arrest for a year. London sent a talented Scottish officer, Lachlan Macquarie, to arrest the rebels. Bligh's career was unblemished by all this – he finished up a vice-admiral – but he lost the governorship of New South Wales to Macquarie.

Macquarie's Vision

Life in the new colony improved under Macquarie's progressive administration and Sydney began to look more like a real town than a military encampment. Thatched huts gave way to properly built schools, churches, a hospital and a courthouse. Francis Greenway, a convicted forger whom Macquarie had pardoned, became the colony's official architect. He turned out to be highly talented. His surviving buildings include St James's Church in King Street and Hyde Park Barracks. Many of Macquarie's reforms were resisted by London, which could not reconcile his civilising efforts with the original concept of creating a hellish environment that filled criminals with dread.

The transportation of prisoners continued halfway into the 19th century, but was eventually outpaced by free immigration. In 1849, when one of the last convict ships docked in Sydney Cove, its presence provoked outrage among Sydney's 'respectable' citizens. The ship arrived at the same time as several other vessels carrying free immigrants. Even so, the descendants of convicts outnumbered free settlers in Sydney until well into the 20th century.

The Gold Rush

In the 19th century, fortune smiled on Australia. In 1813, explorers crossed the Blue Mountains to the west of Sydney and found a land of endless plains – dry country, but arable. In 1851, beyond the Blue Mountains and 200km (130 miles) from Sydney, a veteran of the California gold rush struck gold at a settlement named Ophir.

The gold rush helped shape the history of modern Australia, reversing the exodus of Australians to the California goldfields and bringing an influx of new settlers to the Australian colonies. In 1851, the population of New South Wales was just 187,000. Nine years later it had nearly doubled to 348,000.

Shortly after the Ophir bonanza, prospectors from Melbourne struck gold at Ballarat, triggering an invasion of adventurers from Europe and America, which lifted Australia's population to 1 million by 1860. Life in the goldfields was rough and uncompromising. Miners endured flies, heat, water shortages and extortionate taxes. Hundreds of prospectors arrived in Australia from China, unleashing local racist sentiment, which endured well into the 20th century. Racially based immigration controls – the infamous White Australia Policy – remained in force from 1901 to 1972.

The Bushrangers

Highway robbers, horse thieves and assorted outlaws fanned out across Australia in the 1850s, and the gold rush served to raise the stakes. Among the most notorious was Ned Kelly. A one-time cattle rustler, Kelly's gang pulled off spectacular robberies, mostly in Victoria. His most memorable incursion into New South Wales was in 1879, when the gang kidnapped the population of the town of Jerilderie while trying to make a getaway after a bank robbery. A year later, an unrepentant Ned Kelly went to the gallows. 'Such is life', were Ned's reputed last words.

A Nation Emerges

Australia's island continent remained a collection of separate colonies until 1 January 1901, when Queen Victoria permitted the colonies to unite and form a new nation, the Commonwealth of Australia. The new country bowed to the Queen as head of state, and its final legal authority rested with the British sovereign's private council in London. Although the latter arrangement has changed, Britain's monarch is still Australia's head of state and is depicted on all coinage. Britain's Union Jack flag dominates Australia's flag.

Australia has yet to become a republic, and, in a referendum in 1999, the proposed model for such a state system was rejected, due to concern that it would grant politicians too much power. Australians considered themselves British until well into the 20th century. In World War I, Australian and New Zealand troops formed the Australian and New Zealand Army Corps (Anzac) to fight alongside other British Empire soldiers. On 25 April 1915, the Anzacs landed at Gallipoli (now in Turkey) in an ill-conceived operation that cost the lives of 8,700 Australians, with 19,000 wounded. More than 60,000 Australian soldiers died in World War I, with 152,000 wounded. No other country suffered as high a loss in proportion to its population. The carnage had a major effect on Australia's psyche. Anzac Day, 25 April, is a national day of remembrance.

The Iron Lung

Between the wars, Sydney devoted its energies to building the Harbour Bridge, which gained the nickname 'Iron Lung' because its building took hundreds of workers and kept families breathing (in financial terms) during the Depression.

In World War II, Japanese warplanes repeatedly bombed Darwin in Australia's north, enemy submarines penetrated Sydney Harbour in 1942 and sank a ferry (the torpedo had

The halves of the bridge's arch finally met on 19 August 1930

been fired at an American warship), ships were sunk off the New South Wales coast, and a couple of shells hit Sydney's eastern suburbs. Almost one in three Australians taken prisoner by the Japanese died in captivity. American forces under General Douglas MacArthur arrived in Australia in 1942, and a US force supported by Australia defeated the Japanese decisively in the Battle of the Coral Sea in May of that year.

After the war, Britain aligned itself with Europe and downgraded its ties with the old Empire. As Britain's regional power declined, Australia looked increasingly to the US. Australian troops (over 40,000 of them) fought alongside the US in Vietnam, sparking vehement anti-war protests in Sydney and other Australian cities. Australian Prime Minister Harold Holt promised US President Lyndon B. Johnson that Australia would go 'all the way with LBJ'. The alliance with the US has remained close, and Australia has contributed troops to wars in Iraq and Afghanistan.

A World City

High immigration and rising affluence fed Sydney's postwar expansion. From 1.8 million in 1951, Sydney's population reached 2.7 million in 1971, 3.2 million in 1981, and 4.1 million in 2007. New suburbs were built, especially in the west, while older inner-city districts such as Paddington and Surry Hills declined. From the late 1950s, successive building booms reshaped the CBD and created a mini-CBD at North Sydney. Many historic buildings were demolished, replaced by skyscrapers. Later, the gentrification of inner-city suburbs, led by Paddington in the 1970s, saw the rush to the outer suburbs subside to some extent.

Sydney changed its face, but one building stood out. In 1959, construction of the Sydney Opera House began. Although its architect, Jørn Utzon, resigned in 1966 with the shell incomplete, the building opened to acclaim in 1973.

By the 1980s, Sydney had supplanted Melbourne's role as Australia's main financial centre. Tourism increased significantly, as evidenced by the redevelopment of Darling Harbour in the mid-1980s. Australia's bicentennial celebrations in 1988 focused on Sydney. And the successful staging of the Olympics in 2000 symbolised Sydney's new status as a world city. Although these changes haven't been without cost – disparities between rich and poor have grown, and traffic congestion is increasing – economic conditions, boosted by the Australian mining boom, are good, and Sydney's mood remains buoyant.

Anyone for a cold schooner of the amber nectar?

Historical Landmarks

c.60,000BC Aborigines migrate to Australia from southern Asia.

1606AD Dutch navigator Willem Jansz lands in Cape York.

1688 English pirate William Dampier visits Australia's west coast.

1770 James Cook claims New South Wales for Britain.

1788 First Fleet of British convicts and soldiers arrives.

1808 Governor William Bligh deposed in Rum Rebellion.

1809 Governor Lachlan Macquarie appointed.

1849 Transportation of convicts to New South Wales ends.

1851 Gold discovered near Bathurst.

1860s Melbourne overtakes Sydney as Australia's largest city.

1898 Queen Victoria Building completed.

1901 Britain allows its Australian colonies to unify into one nation.

1905 Sydney overtakes Melbourne as Australia's largest city.

1913 Construction of Canberra commences.

1915 Anzac soldiers storm ashore at Gallipoli in military disaster.

1932 Height of the Great Depression (unemployment rate is 32 percent); Sydney Harbour Bridge opens.

1942 Japanese midget submarines penetrate Sydney Harbour.

1946 Australia conceives 'Populate or Perish' immigration programme.

1955 Arrival of Australia's one-millionth postwar migrant.

1962 Aborigines given right to vote in federal elections.

1965 Australia enters Vietnam War.

1973 Sydney Opera House opens.

1975 Governor General (Queen's representative in Australia) sacks Australia's elected Prime Minister.

1988 Bicentenary of arrival of First Fleet.

1995 Sydney opens its first legal casino.

2000 Sydney Olympic and Paralympic Games.

2001 Centenary of Federation.

2003 Australia sends troops to war in Iraq.

2004 Aborigines fight police in inner-city Redfern.

2008 Federal government apologizes to Aborigines for past wrongs.

and boisterous; others are secluded and little known, found only after hiking along wooded trails. The beaches can be divided into two main types: ocean beaches, which face out to sea and have stronger surf; and harbour beaches, which line Sydney Harbour and tend to be more tranquil.

Sydneysiders

At work or play, Sydneysiders are a friendly and informal bunch. Old class distinctions were largely wiped out by the harsh realities of the colony's early history, where a person's skills and abilities became more important than anything else. However, beneath their 'no worries' approach, Sydneysiders have energy, ambition, belief and an overwhelming pride in their city. In the 1970s, when development projects threatened some of the city's most cherished historic or environmentally sensitive sites, builders' unions instituted

Sydneysiders enjoying beach life

The harbour bisects Sydney; the CBD is on the south side

The Outdoor Life

Sydneysiders (as the city's residents are known) make the most of their favourable surroundings and climate and delight in outdoor activities. The city's sports facilities are top class and received a further boost when Sydney hosted the Olympics in 2000. Sydneysiders play and watch a panoply of sports including cricket, rugby league, Aussie Rules football, horseracing, swimming, surfing and yachting.

If you enjoy beach life, Sydney is for you. The shoreline is convoluted and would extend for some 350km (218 miles) if drawn out in a straight line. Along the coast and within the harbour, the city has dozens of beaches, all of which are open to the public. The beaches occupy a special position in the Sydney psyche and each has a distinct character. Some attract families, picnickers, frisbee throwers and volleyball players, others draw dedicated surfers, one or two are frequented by furtive (or not so furtive) nudists. Some beaches are crowded

WHERE TO GO

Sydney is a big, sprawling city. It stretches some 75km (45 miles) from north to south and 65km (40 miles) from east to west. Fortunately for visitors, most of Sydney's essential sights are grouped conveniently close together, just south of the Harbour Bridge. As well as the bridge itself, these include The Rocks, the Sydney Opera House, the Royal Botanic Gardens, the CBD and Darling Harbour. All are accessible on foot or by monorail, bus or train.

A short bus or train ride gets you to the trendy neighbourhoods of the Inner West, and the beaches (including Bondi), café culture and shopping opportunities of the Eastern Suburbs. Circular Quay, also south of the bridge, is the main ferry terminal, and a jumping-off point for exploring the wonders of Sydney Harbour.

Accessible by train or on organised tour are western Sydney's Olympic Park (site of the 2000 Olympics), Featherdale Wildlife Park and Parramatta, which can also be reached by ferry. Sights to the north accessible by ferry or bus include Taronga Zoo, Manly and the Northern Beaches.

Sydney has several great natural attractions on its doorstep. The Blue Mountains, about 100km (60 miles) to the west, make an unmissable daytrip, either by car, train or as part of an organised tour. Those with time to spare might also like to consider an excursion to the Jenolan Caves, the Hunter Valley, the Southern Highlands and the Hawkesbury River.

Also included in this book is Canberra, about 300km (185 miles) southwest of Sydney, which is Australia's capital city and the location of some of the country's premier galleries and museums.

The best views of the bridge and opera house are from the water

SYDNEY HARBOUR

The harbour is the city's essence – spanned by the great bridge and adorned by the shell-like sails of Sydney Opera House. Sydneysiders flock to the harbour to celebrate great events. They turned out here to greet Queen Elizabeth II on her first visit to Australia in 1954, and they were here again in January 1988 to celebrate the bicentenary of the First Fleet's arrival, which marked the founding of modern Australia.

New Year celebrations, sometimes tumultuous, take place in the historic Rocks area near the southern end of Sydney Harbour Bridge each year. Tens of thousands of people turn out to watch a massive fireworks display that has the bridge as its focal point. Each Boxing Day, thousands of Sydneysiders line the harbour to watch the start of the gruelling Sydney to Hobart yacht race.

The best way to see **Sydney Harbour** is to get out on to it. Fortunately, doing just that has always been easy – Sydney Ferries runs numerous public ferries from Circular Quay (called Sydney Cove in the days of convict settlement), providing a fast and cheap means of seeing the city's most attractive aspects. In addition to being vital links for commuters, the ferries and high-speed JetCat catamarans are bargains for tourists. Sydney Ferries also operates morning, afternoon and evening cruises around the harbour. A number of private companies also offer cruises on vessels that run the gamut from large cruisers to a mock paddle wheeler. Itineraries range from hour-long 'best of' trips to lunch and dinner cruises and overnight excursions. One of the leading tour

Aerial views

One way to see the harbour at its best is to fly over it. A number of companies offer scenic flights. Try Sydney Helicopters (tel: 02 9637-4455) or Sydney by Seaplane (tel: 1300-656-787).

Approaching Circular Quay on a ferry

boat companies is Captain Cook Cruises (www.captaincook.com.au; tel: 02 9296 1111). You can also set sail on a tall ship (www.sydneytallships.com.au; tel: 1300-664-410) or go for an invigorating spin on a fast jet boat (www.harbourjet.com; tel: 1300-887-373, or www.ozjetboating.com; tel: 02 9808-3700).

Harbour Highlights

Exploring Sydney Harbour is as easy as hopping on a ferry. Popular destinations include Taronga Zoo *(see page 28)*, Cremorne Point *(see page 29)*, Darling Harbour *(see page 48)*, Balmain *(see page 61)*, Parramatta *(see page 63)*, Watsons Bay *(see page 69)* and Manly *(see page 70)*.

Sydney Harbour National Park fringes a long stretch of the northern side of the harbour and also includes some harbour islands and a chunk of the southern foreshore. Walking tracks lead through bushland remnants, past waterfront mansions and along harbour beaches.

Koala at Taronga Zoo

Fort Denison, part of Sydney Harbour National Park, occupies a small harbour island known as 'Pinchgut', which originally served as a prison. Troublesome convicts endured a bread-and-water diet and sometimes even worse. In 1796, a murderer was executed by hanging on the island and his body gibbeted for three years as a warning. Fort Denison contains a martello tower (a circular masonry blockhouse), a barracks and gun battery, all dating from the 1850s. The fort is open for guided tours only (tel: 02 9247-5033).

Also part of the national park is **Shark Island**, off Rose Bay, which offers shady picnic areas and grand harbour views. You can reach it by a regular weekend ferry service, Sundays only in winter (tel: 02 9247-5033).

The ferry ride from Circular Quay to **Taronga Zoo** (daily 9am–5pm; charge; www.zoo.nsw.gov.au) is pleasant and takes only about 12 minutes. Most tourists view their first kangaroos and koalas at the zoo, situated in natural bushland at Bradleys Head, Mosman. The setting can't be beaten: if you choose your vantage point carefully, you can photograph the heads of giraffes against a background of the CBD cityscape, including the Opera House.

Designers at the zoo have worked to ensure that the animals live in sympathetic surroundings reminiscent of their natural habitats. The Nocturnal House features indigenous night-time creatures illuminated in artificial moonlight, unaware of onlookers. The Rainforest Aviary houses hundreds of tropical birds. Wild Asia recreates an Asian rainforest and features a walk-through aviary and animals such as tapirs, gibbons and otters. A new aquatic area is under construction. If you arrange your visit around feeding times, which are on the website, you can watch the keepers distribute food while they deliver talks about their charges. The zoo has an active educational programme and there's even a seal show.

Other parts of Sydney Harbour worth seeing are **Balmoral Beach**, near Mosman, reached by bus 247 from the Queen Victoria Building, and **Kirribilli**, just across the harbour from Circular Quay and accessible by ferry, train (to Milsons Point station) or on foot across the Harbour Bridge.

One particularly lovely short walk on the Lower North Shore starts from the ferry wharf at **Cremorne Point** – where there are fine views of the city and harbour – and winds along the shore of Mosman Bay to the wharf at Mosman. The walk takes about 1½ hours.

Weird Waddlers

The Echidna and Platypus House at Taronga Zoo allows you to view these reclusive Australian monotremes (egg-laying mammals) close-up. The waddling, spine-covered echidnas dine on ants and termites. The duck-billed platypus is even more peculiar, having astonished observers since explorers first laid eyes on it. When 18th-century zoologists in London received their first stuffed and preserved specimens, they doubted anything that weird could exist. Most experts considered it a composite fake, assembled by Chinese taxidermists for sale to gullible seafarers. The platypus is the size of a small cat, with a broad bill and webbed feet like a duck. It is amphibious, covered in fine fur, possesses milk-secreting glands, lays eggs and dines exclusively on mud, from which it extracts tiny plants and animals. The platypus was not declared a mammal until 1884.

Aboriginal buskers at Circular Quay

HARBOURSIDE ATTRACTIONS

Circular Quay and The Rocks

Circular Quay is frequented by buskers, artists, and a few 'living statues' who appear to be cast in bronze or aluminium – until they move, that is. Circular Quay railway station provides quick connections to Kings Cross and to points in the centre of the city, as well as to the outlying suburbs. The Quay (as it's often called) is a major bus terminal and an easy place to hail a cab.

> **The Rocks**, just west of Circular Quay, is touristy and souvenir-dominated in some parts, quaint and fascinating in others. The birthplace of Sydney – the First Fleet ended its journey from England here in 1788 – this district was a squalid slum in the 19th century, harbouring an evil gang of cutthroats known as The Rocks Push. Many of the district's original houses were torn down in 1900, when the area was hit

by an outbreak of bubonic plague. It killed nearly 100 people. Plenty of historic buildings survived, only to be threatened in the 1960s by developers wanting to level the whole place and replace it with high-rise buildings. A 'Save The Rocks' campaign, backed by the union movement, only just prevailed.

It's worth visiting the **Sydney Visitor Centre** (daily 9.30am–5.30pm), corner of Argyle and Playfair streets, before setting out to explore. Displays and pamphlets provide insights into the area's history. **Cadman's Cottage** (110 George Street) is The Rocks' oldest house, a simple stone cottage built in 1816 and occupied for many years by the governor's boat crew. John Cadman, a pardoned convict, was the original coxswain. The cottage is now the Sydney Harbour National Park information centre (Mon–Fri 9.30am–4.30pm, Sat–Sun 10am–4.30pm). A former police station at 127 George Street is decorated with what is perhaps one of the most telling reminders of the convict era – a stone lion's head wearing an imperial crown and clenching a police-issue truncheon in its jaws.

A short stroll from the visitor centre, the **Museum of Contemporary Art** (daily 10am–5pm; free; www.mca.com.au) gives new life to an Art Deco building formerly used by the Maritime Services Board. Few other art museums enjoy such a view. Displays change regularly at the museum, and the café on the terrace facing Circular Quay and the harbour is excellent (*see page 137*).

Walking north from Cadman's Cottage up Argyle Street you arrive at the so-

Museum of Contemporary Art

Notorious Argyle

The Argyle Cut was a notorious hang-out of thugs until the early 1900s, when slum clearance after the bubonic plague reduced criminal activities in the area.

called **Argyle Cut**, a road carved through sandstone cliffs. It was started in 1843 by convict gangs using pick-axes and finished 18 years later by non-convict labour using explosives. At the top of Argyle Cut, Cumberland Street provides access to Sydney Harbour Bridge via Cumberland Steps. Beer connoisseurs will enjoy the range of beers available at the bar at the Australian Hotel, 100 Cumberland Street *(see page 102 for details)*.

A little further on, in Argyle Place, you will find a neat row of terraced houses straight out of Georgian England. This area is called Millers Point and, with its tree-lined streets, street-corner pubs and old houses, has a less touristy, more relaxed feel to it than The Rocks. Three grand old pubs in this area deserve mention. The quaint Hero of Waterloo at 81 Lower Fort Street was built on top of a maze of subterranean cellars to which drunken patrons were lured, to be sold as crew members to unscrupulous sea captains. That practice has died out but the cellars remain. The Lord Nelson, a square sandstone block of a building at the corner of Kent and Argyle streets, was built about 1840 and has maintained a British naval atmosphere ever since. It brews its own beers, some of them pretty strong. Old Admiral ale has an alcoholic strength of 6.7 percent. The Palisade Hotel at 35 Bettington Street was built later than the other two establishments, but retains a pleasant colonial atmosphere, enhanced by expansive harbour views and a fine restaurant.

For history without the refreshments, visit the **Garrison Church**, officially named the Holy Trinity Anglican Church, which dates from the early 1840s. As the unofficial name indicates, it was the church for members of the garrison regiment, the men in charge of the convict colony. It's now a fashionable place to get married.

To the left of the church, up a flight of stone stairs, is Observatory Park, which gives views to Darling Harbour and Balmain. **Sydney Observatory**, built of sandstone in the 1850s, was once the headquarters of the Government Astronomer, and now houses displays on astronomy. Walk north down Lower Fort Street and you will come to Dawes Point Park, beneath the arch of the Harbour Bridge. Go down to the harbour foreshore for views, and then follow the foreshore around to the converted cargo wharves of **Walsh Bay**, a fast-growing residential and cultural area, home to the Sydney Theatre and the Wharf Theatre.

Victorian buildings, The Rocks

Back down at the start of George Street, close to the Irish-influenced Mercantile Hotel, **The Rocks Market** takes place each Saturday and Sunday under a long sail-like canopy. Musical groups and street entertainers perform, while numerous stallholders sell crafts, leatherwear, souvenirs, toys and gifts. Further up towards the bridge, the Customs Officers Stairs lead down to some charming harbourside restaurants housed in old bond stores, fronting Campbells Cove.

Sydney Harbour Bridge

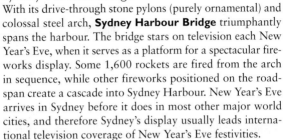

With its drive-through stone pylons (purely ornamental) and colossal steel arch, **Sydney Harbour Bridge** triumphantly spans the harbour. The bridge stars on television each New Year's Eve, when it serves as a platform for a spectacular fireworks display. Some 1,600 rockets are fired from the arch in sequence, while other fireworks positioned on the road-span create a cascade into Sydney Harbour. New Year's Eve arrives in Sydney before it does in most other major world cities, and therefore Sydney's display usually leads international television coverage of New Year's Eve festivities.

Before the Sydney Opera House opened in 1973, the bridge was the most internationally recognised symbol of Sydney. Completed in 1932, the bridge was to have been opened by the Premier of New South Wales, but just as that worthy gentleman approached the official ribbon brandishing his pair of golden scissors, an unauthorised horseman rode through the crowd and slashed the ribbon in two with a sabre. The mounted protestor, a member of a right-wing paramilitary group, declared the bridge open in the name of 'the decent citizens of New South Wales'. It was a bizarre initiation for a Sydney icon

Traversing the Bridge

Before the Sydney Harbour Bridge was built, the city's North Shore could be reached only by ferry, and ferry services were stretched to capacity. The cost of building the bridge has long since been met, but a road toll remains in place. If you cross the bridge in a taxi, the $3 toll is added to your fare. For a pleasant short excursion, catch a train from Wynyard to Milsons Point on the North Shore. This 5-minute trip of just one stop involves a scenic journey across the bridge. Alight at Milsons Point and walk back across the bridge, using the footway on the bridge's eastern side. The views are sensational.

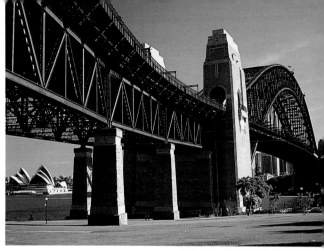

Sydney Harbour Bridge

that was intended to be the world's longest single-span bridge – it was beaten just four months before its opening by New York's Bayonne Bridge, which is just 63cm (2ft) longer.

Sydney Harbour Bridge, which took nine years to build, was one of the foremost engineering feats of its day. Some 1,400 workers toiled on the 503-m (1,651-ft) structure. Sixteen lost their lives. Repainting the bridge is a 10-year job, using 30,000 litres (almost 7,000 UK gallons) of paint. Once finished, it's time to start again. Paul 'Crocodile Dundee' Hogan worked on this monotonous task for years before discovering there was more money – and more satisfaction – in show business.

Nicknamed the 'Coathanger', the bridge is equipped with a cycle lane (on the western side), as well as a walkway, road lanes and a railway line. For a small fee, you can climb the 200 stairs inside the south-east pylon for panoramic views (daily 10am–5pm; charge). There's a little museum there, too. The stairs are reached via Cumberland Street in the Rocks.

The bridge's role is less crucial now that you can drive under the harbour through a tunnel. The tunnel trip is faster but boring. Guided climbing tours of the bridge now allow you to walk right over the huge over-arching span *(see page 89)*.

For a nice scenic walk, cross over the bridge to the delightful harbourside suburb of **Kirribilli**, whose tree-lined streets – some of which face the Opera House – invite exploration. Refresh yourself in one of the numerous cafés and restaurants here before returning to the city.

Sydney Opera House

Standing on the western side of Circular Quay and gazing east, the viewer is confronted by one of Sydney's most beautiful buildings, the **Sydney Opera House** (www.sydney operahouse.com). Covered in a million gleaming white tiles, this extraordinary building does the seemingly impossible

Sunset at the Sydney Opera House

and embellishes a perfect harbour. While it's hard to imagine the harbour without it, the Opera House nearly wasn't built at all. The design was one of 233 entries submitted in a contest to find an ideal building for the site, which had previously been occupied by a squat, turreted depot for trams.

As the contest progressed, several banal entries (including one resembling two giant shoeboxes) were short-listed. Danish architect Jørn Utzon's vision for the site, the eventual winner, was at first discarded. Fortunately, Utzon's plan was spotted by accident in a pile of rejects by US architect Eero Saarinen, one of the judges. Saarinen recognised the plan's potential and brought it to the attention of his colleagues.

Utzon moved to Sydney to oversee construction, but endless bickering with petty officials and enormous cost over-runs took their toll and he resigned from the project in 1966, returning disillusioned to Denmark. The interior plan was subsequently handed over to a committee of Australian architects. Utzon has never returned to see the finished work.

In 1999 he agreed to be a consultant with his architect son, Jan, in drawing up a statement of design principles that will help guide Australian architect Richard Johnson on future development works. The first fruits of that partnership are the Utzon Room (2004), used for functions and small-scale concerts, and a 45-m (150-ft) colonnade along the Harbour Bridge side of the Opera House, opened in 2006. Utzon has also submitted plans for an ambitious refurbishment of the interior of the main performance halls, but the price tag – A$700 million – may prove too much for the building's owner, the New South Wales Government.

The Opera House was originally budgeted at A$7 million, but ended up costing 13 times that. In true Sydney style, the shortfall was raised by a lottery. Despite its cost, the finished project was immediately hailed for its grace, taste and class. Elegance extends from the tip of its highest shell-like roof, which soars 67m (221ft), to the Drama Theatre's orchestra pit, situated several metres below sea level.

Strictly speaking, the term Opera House is a misnomer. The building's opera theatre (seating 1,547) is fairly small and not entirely satisfactory, although its intimacy helps some productions. Its concert hall (seating 2,697) is the biggest of five halls, and stages rock and jazz concerts as well as classical music. The Opera House offers two restaurants: Guillaume at Bennelong and Bistro Mozart. It's worth taking a guided tour of the whole building. The one-hour tours depart every 30 minutes from 9am to 5pm each day, except for Christmas Day and Good Friday (no need to book).

Back towards Circular Quay is the colonnaded Opera Quays pedestrian link between Circular Quay and the Opera House. The cafés, restaurants, shops and art-house cinema lining the way are lively additions to the Sydney scene.

Royal Botanic Gardens

Situated next to the Opera House, Sydney's lush **Royal Botanic Gardens** (established in 1816) offer an extensive collection of Pacific plant life, a tropical garden, palm grove,

Bats in Procession

The large flocks of bats you may see flitting through Sydney skies are called grey-headed flying-foxes. Weighing up to 1kg (2.2 pounds) each and known to scientists as *Pteropus poliocephalus*, the bats fly over the city at dusk to dine on figs and other soft fruit. Watching a flock on the wing, silhouetted against an awesome orange and mauve sunset, is one of Sydney's priceless experiences. The bats, with their furry, foxy faces, frequent the Royal Botanic Gardens (especially the palm grove) and Centennial Park, but their main camp is at Gordon, a leafy suburb on Sydney's North Shore.

There are over 45,000 plants in the Royal Botanic Gardens

lawns, a pretty little restaurant tucked away in the greenery and some wonderful picnic spots (daily 7am–sunset; www. rbgsyd.nsw.gov.au). A sign in the gardens is worth quoting: 'Please walk on the grass. We also invite you to smell the roses, hug the trees, talk to the birds, sit on the benches and picnic on the lawns. This is your Garden, and unlike most botanic gardens overseas, admission to the Royal Botanic Gardens is free.' (A slot for donations is provided in case you are inspired to generosity.) There are free daily guided walking tours (at 10.30am) or you can pay to go on the trackless train, which winds its way through the gardens.

Sublime views of Sydney Harbour can be enjoyed in the Royal Botanic Gardens from **Mrs Macquarie's Chair**, a sandstone rock ledge carved in 1816 for the wife of Sydney's best-loved governor. Mrs Macquarie's Chair stands beside Mrs Macquarie's Road on Mrs Macquarie's Point. (You couldn't go far wrong in early 19th-century Sydney by naming geographical features after the governor's wife.) The view from Mrs Macquarie's Chair, looking west across Farm Cove to the Opera House, is one of the world's most photographed. Here, nature and architecture meld beautifully, with the Royal Botanic Gardens forming a perfect backdrop to the Opera House.

Beside the gardens, and separated from them by the Cahill Expressway, is **The Domain**, another of Sydney's wonderful open spaces. Given over to amateur orators on Sundays (rather like Speakers' Corner in London's Hyde Park), The Domain is also home to the **Art Gallery of New South Wales** (daily 10am–5pm, until 9pm Wed; free; www.art gallery.nsw.gov.au). The original building, dating from 1897, has a formal exterior decorated with much bronze statuary; light-infused modern extensions provide sweeping views of east Sydney, part of the harbour, and the suburb of Woolloomooloo. (A spelling teaser for Sydney schoolchildren, Woolloomooloo was threatened by wholesale demolition in the 1970s, but was saved by resident protests and union 'green bans'.) An afternoon at the art gallery will give you a crash course in more than a century of the best of traditional and modern Australian art. The Yiribana Gallery there is devoted to Aboriginal art and Torres Strait Islander art. The Asian and South Pacific sections are also impressive. The gallery stages regular exhibitions of Australian and foreign artists, and there are free guided tours of the collection on most days. When you need a break, a café and restaurant await, where you can sit down and admire the harbour views.

Finger Wharf

From the rear of the Art Gallery of New South Wales there are good views of the Woolloomooloo Finger Wharf, an old cargo wharf that has been converted into apartments, restaurants and an upmarket hotel. Look out for actor Russell Crowe, one of the wharf's residents.

CENTRAL SYDNEY

Sydney's city centre, universally called the **CBD** (for Central Business District), includes a magnificently restored late 19th-century emporium, several elegant Georgian sandstone edifices, some fine Victorian structures, and a vast number of high-rise buildings. A few recent skyscrapers are notable and some are even elegant, but most belong to the so-called 'international eggcrate' school of architecture – bland modern buildings that were erected mainly in the 1960s and 1970s.

Sydney Tower

George, Pitt and Market Streets

George Street, running north–south, is the city's main thoroughfare. Parallel to it is Pitt Street, which is pedestrian-only between Market and Castlereagh streets. Together, this area makes up Sydney's main shopping district. Myer, one of the main department stores, is in **Pitt Street Mall**, and David Jones, the other department store chain, is nearby. Shopping complexes include the Imperial Arcade, Centrepoint, Skygarden and Glasshouse. The **Strand Arcade**, which runs between Pitt Street Mall and George Street, is a Victorian shopping arcade with some very up-to-the-minute boutiques.

At 305m (1,000ft), the **Sydney Tower** at Centrepoint is the city's highest vantage point. From this 1970s pinnacle

Stained glass in the QVB

visitors have a superb 360-degree view of Sydney and its surroundings. On a clear day you can spot Terrigal Beach, 100km (62 miles) north, and the Blue Mountains far to the west. The tower is a little shorter the Eiffel Tower. Sydney's version is unusual in that it has no communications function. It houses a revolving restaurant, a show on the history of Sydney and an observation deck. For an even better view, you might like to try the Skywalk, in which you walk outside Sydney Tower's turret *(see page 89)*.

Walk north on George or Pitt streets to reach the city's main square, **Martin Place**, flanked by the imposing Victorian Renaissance-style General Post Office (GPO) building. No longer a working post office, this structure has been converted into a 418-room, five-star Westin hotel, with luxury and designer shops, and upmarket restaurants, cafés and bars. During World War II, the GPO's clock tower was dismantled for fear that Japanese bombers might zero in on the landmark; it was restored 20 years later.

From the same era as the GPO, but even grander, the **Queen Victoria Building** (QVB) occupies an entire block on George Street opposite Sydney Town Hall. The Byzantine-style QVB began as a municipal market and commercial centre, including a hotel and a concert hall, topped by statuary and 21 domes. Built in 1898 to commemorate Queen Victoria's Golden Jubilee, this splendid building was later downgraded into offices and a library. In the 1960s, small-minded officials decided to demolish the QVB to make way for a car park. Fortunately, the authorities ran short of money, the demolition was put on hold and the building was spared the wrecker's ball. It was faithfully restored in the 1980s to create a magnificent all-weather shopping centre housing nearly 200 chic boutiques, cafés and restaurants, in a cool and unhurried atmosphere of period charm. There are several good cafés here that are worth trying, including The Tearoom on Level 3 which serves acclaimed morning and afternoon teas.

Opposite the QVB on George Street is the Hilton Hotel. Although the modern concrete-and-glass Hilton building is no rival to the elegant sandstone lady across the road, it does contain a hidden architectural gem in its basement. This is the **Marble Bar**, a Beaux-Arts masterpiece of a pub, much older than the Hilton itself. A cornucopia of Victorian paintings, stained glass, marble and mirrors, the Marble Bar was preserved when the 19th-century building it was part of was knocked down to make way for the Hilton in the 1970s.

Paddy's Market and Chinatown

Chinatown, at the southern end of Sydney's CBD, is the home of Paddy's Market, over 150 years old but now housed in a new purpose-built venue. Paddy's is a mecca for weekend bargain hunters. More than 1,000 stalls sell everything from fish, mangoes, Chinese herbs and sacks of onions to T-shirts, hot dogs, watches, shoes, jewellery and souvenirs. It's open Thur–Mon 9am–5pm. Chinatown is full of inexpensive eating houses. At large Asian emporiums there, numerous food outlets share the same seating, crockery, chopsticks and cutlery. Thai, Cambodian, Chinese, Japanese and Malaysian cuisine are all served in adjoining food booths. A tasty bargain.

State Library of New South Wales

Macquarie's Sydney

The CBD's only real boulevard is **Macquarie Street**, laid out by Governor Lachlan Macquarie and running from East Circular Quay near the Opera House to Hyde Park. This relatively short street, filled with historic buildings, is well worth the walk.

Starting at the northern end, Macquarie Street flanks **Government House**, open from Friday to Sunday for guided tours (tel: 02 9931-5222). This extraordinary mock-Gothic castle, complete with crenellated battlements, was designed in 1834 by Edward Blore, architect to King William IV. Until 1996 it was the official residence of the Governor of New South Wales. Continuing south along Macquarie Street brings you past the Sir Stamford at Circular Quay Hotel on the right-hand side (formerly Sydney's venereal disease clinic) and BMA House, a splendid Art-Deco edifice.

Just off Macquarie Street, nestled beneath a modern skyscraper, is the **Museum of Sydney** (daily 9.30am–5pm; charge), built on the site of the colony's first Government House. This small museum's permanent exhibits focus on the city's history, from 1788 onwards, and regular temporary exhibitions are also staged. There's an excellent café adjoining the museum.

The **State Library of New South Wales**, bordering the Domain, consists of two buildings, one old, one new, linked by a walkway. Classical columns announce the main portal of the old Mitchell Wing, built in Greek-revival style in the early 20th century, while the adjoining 1988 concrete-and-glass addition boosts the building's size and spirits. The next building is **State Parliament House**, an elegantly colonnaded building that has resounded with political debates (and much invective, not all of it sober), since 1827. It's open for visits and admission is free.

Sydney Hospital superseded the Rum Hospital of the early colonial days *(see box on page 16)*. Built in the 1880s, it is the oldest hospital in Australia. Outside stands a bronze statue of **Il Porcellino**, a wild boar, a replica of a 17th-century original in Florence. The statue was donated by an Italian immigrant whose relatives had worked at the hospital. Patting its snout is said to bring good luck. Just inside the hospital grounds, a curious green-and-yellow fountain embellished with brightly coloured flamingos and swans is intended, presumably, to lift the spirits of recovering patients.

The **Mint** (Mon–Fri 9am–5pm; free) next door, originally the Rum Hospital's south wing, was converted into a mint to process gold-rush bullion midway through the 19th century. In the early days it was used to produce 'holey dollars' – Spanish coins recycled to ease a desperate shortage of cash. It ceased operating as a mint in 1926, and now houses a small display on the site's history.

Outside the Museum of Sydney

Immediately opposite, a huge brown block-like building houses the **State and**

Commonwealth Law Courts. This modern contribution to Macquarie Street, out of scale with the opposite side of the street, is adorned with Australia's coat of arms – an emu and kangaroo each trying to look fierce. The forecourt is enlivened at times by the arrival of barristers in gowns and wigs.

Hyde Park Barracks (daily 9.30am–5pm; charge), next to the Mint, was commissioned by Governor Macquarie to house 600 male convicts. It was designed by Francis Greenway, pardoned forger and architectural genius. Completed in 1819 and adorned with a fine colonial clock, this is perhaps the best Georgian building in Sydney. At various times it housed 'unprotected females' and Irish orphans.

The barracks is now a museum of Sydney's early days, with an emphasis on giving an insight into the lives of convicts. A convict dormitory with hammocks has been reconstructed on the third floor. A computer base gives public access to the records of every prisoner who passed through the institution. (More detailed records, covering virtually everyone ever transported to Australia, are available at the State Library of NSW, a few blocks further down Macquarie Street.) In addition, there are displays of photographs, pictures, letters and objects dating from the convict period.

Hyde Park, at the end of Macquarie Street, is a fraction the size of its London namesake, but it provides the same green relief. The land was cleared at the beginning of the 19th century, with a racetrack being its first big attraction. Hyde Park was the venue for boxing matches, and was also the new colony's first cricket pitch. The two most formal features of these 16-hectare (40-acre) gardens are the

War mementos

Pine trees around Hyde Park's Anzac War Memorial were grown from seeds gathered at Gallipoli in Turkey, where soldiers from the Australian and New Zealand Corps (Anzac) fought in 1915.

Anzac War Memorial, commemorating the country's war dead, and the **Archibald Fountain**, an extravaganza of statuary on mythical themes, with a fine plume of water.

Sightseers who enjoy old places of worship should mark three targets on the edge of Hyde Park. To the north, the early colonial **St James's Church** on Queen's Square was designed by Francis Greenway as a courthouse and consecrated in 1824. When its use was changed, the intended cells were converted into a crypt. Across College Street to the east, twin-spired **St Mary's Cathedral** stands on the

Anzac War Memorial

site of the colony's first Catholic church, and from the same era, the magnificent **Great Synagogue** faces the park from the opposite side, across Elizabeth Street.

The **Australian Museum** (daily 9.30am–5pm; charge; www.austmus.gov.au) on College Street facing Hyde Park, was established in 1827, soon after settlement, largely so scientists could show off Australia's unique flora and fauna. Distinguished architecturally by massive Corinthian pillars, the museum is still strong on natural history. You can learn about Australian birds and insects, view some local dinosaurs, and see Aboriginal artefacts. This rather stuffy, old-fashioned establishment is undergoing renovation, and some exhibition halls may be closed to the public.

The monorail links Darling Harbour to the CBD

DARLING HARBOUR

Darling Harbour, a vast tourist and leisure centre built by decree in time for the 1988 Bicentennial celebrations, offers parks, a light and airy shopping complex, the Convention and Exhibition Centre, restaurants and museums.

Despite its proximity to Sydney's centre, Darling Harbour has never been fully integrated with the central city. It lies alongside the CBD like an island. Linking the CBD with Darling Harbour's diverse elements is the **Monorail**, whose elevated track covers a 3.5-km (2-mile) loop of eight stations. Dubbed the 'Monsterail' during construction, this conveyance has always been controversial; critics consider its track and pillars a blot on the cityscape. Views from the Monorail are vastly preferable to views of it. While the Monorail is seriously flawed as a public transport system, it's an amusing sightseeing vehicle, resembling the one at

Disneyland. A recorded commentary with an advertising theme tells you where you are.

To reach Darling Harbour from the city, you are probably better off walking across Pyrmont Bridge, which runs off the end of Market Street. The 1902 bridge, along which the Monorail runs, is constructed of wood and was the first electrically operated swing-span bridge in the world.

Where to Eat and Shop

On the western side of Darling Harbour, Harbourside Shopping Centre offers more than 200 shops and food outlets. Shops sell gemstones, clothing, souvenirs, gifts, Aboriginal art and much more. Dining options range from cheap and cheerful snacks to stylish seafood dining at Jordons.

Diagonally opposite on the eastern side of Darling Harbour is **Cockle Bay Wharf**, a more upmarket development. Cockle Bay features five-star eateries, little cafés and coffee shops, and a pub, Pontoon. The fine-dining restaurants include Nick's Seafood and Coast (both are seafood restaurants), and Chinta Ria Temple of Love.

On the other side of Pyrmont Bridge is the ferry wharf and Sydney Aquarium *(see page 52)*, beyond which is **King Street Wharf**. Eateries here range from the inexpensive Wagamama and Malaya to the more upmarket Essence.

Main Attractions

Next to Harbourside Shopping Centre, the **Australian National Maritime Museum** (daily 9.30am–5pm; free; www.anmm.gov.au) attracts more than 120,000 international visitors a year. Housed in a large white building with a wave-form roof, the museum displays more than 2,000 maritime objects in permanent and temporary exhibitions. Moored at wharves outside is the museum's fleet of 14 historic vessels, including a submarine and a replica of Cook's ship, the *Endeavour*.

The **Imax Theatre** in Darling Harbour has one of the world's largest screens, 10 times larger than those found in traditional cinemas. The ground floor features a retail store with an Australian-inspired selection of gifts and merchandise, and there's a mezzanine bar with a view of the Sydney skyline.

Darling Harbour's Exhibition Centre is designed on the suspension bridge principle, with cables attached to masts holding up the roofs. Outside it, **Tumbalong Park** offers open spaces, brilliantly original fountains, geometrical challenges, swings, slides and mazes.

At the western end of Darling Harbour is the circular concrete **Sydney Entertainment Centre**. Designed for sports

The Chinese Garden

events, concerts and other public festivities, it can hold 12,500 spectators. Next door is the **Pumphouse**, which serves as a tavern for thirsty tourists. Not far from here is the **Powerhouse Museum** (daily 10am–5pm; charge; www.power housemuseum.com), which focuses on science and design. Its hands-on exhibits are popular with children.

Darling Harbour's **Chinese Garden** was a joint effort by the governments of New South Wales and the Chinese province of Guangdong. This 1-hectare (2.5-acre) garden allows quiet contemplation amid apricot, azalea, jasmine and weeping willow trees overhanging paths, ponds and rock formations.

Nearby is the **Outback Centre** (daily 10am–7pm; free; www.outbackcentre.com.au), which attracts overseas visitors and Australians alike by providing a look at Aboriginal art and life. The centre contains a gallery, theatre and shop. The gallery's collection of canvases, prints, ceramics and fibre art comes from artists in Aboriginal communities across Australia. If you want to learn more about Aboriginal art, go to the free half-hour 'Art of the Outback' lecture daily at 4pm. Another popular attraction in the centre's theatre is 'Sounds of the Outback', a live performance of didgeridoo music. Performances take place at 1, 3 and 5pm daily. The centre's shop has a very large range of souvenirs and gifts, from didgeridoos and boomerangs to books, posters and toiletries.

Come face-to-face with large sharks at the Sydney Aquarium

Sydney Aquarium (daily 10am–10pm; charge; www.sydneyaquarium.com.au) on the city side of Darling Harbour, is one of the largest aquariums in the world, and one of the city's biggest attractions. There are hundreds of aquatic species here, including fish, sharks, crocodiles, turtles, eels, jellyfish, seals, penguins and platypus. Perhaps start with the crocodiles, whose baleful immobility seems to challenge crowds to hang around until one of them stirs. Or head first to the Open Ocean Oceanarium, where you can go face-to-face with sharks that weigh up to 300kg (660lbs) and measure over 9m (30ft) long. The aquarium has 146m (480ft) of see-through underwater tunnels. You can also walk around a natural-style seal sanctuary outside. A major attraction is the Great Barrier Reef Complex, which is home to an oceanarium, live coral caves, a coral atoll and a tropical touch-pool; in total, the complex houses over 6,000 animals from the Great Barrier Reef off Australia's northeastern coast. There are regular feeding times throughout the week, usually at mid-morning and mid-afternoon.

Adjacent to the aquarium is **Sydney Wildlife World** (daily 9am–10pm; www.sydneywildlifeworld.com.au; charge). This mini-zoo has a fine selection of Australian fauna, including spiders, snakes, lizards, parrots, wallabies, and wombats. The star attractions, however, are the koalas. You can visit Wildlife World and the aquarium on a joint ticket.

EASTERN SUBURBS

Kings Cross

Bright lights and shady characters exist side by side in Kings Cross, a couple of railway stops from Circular Quay. 'The Cross', as it's often called, is Sydney's version of Paris's Pigalle or London's Soho – neon-filled, a bit tacky, crawling with hedonists and counter-culturalists of all persuasions. Action continues 24 hours a day, with a diverting cavalcade of humanity: the bizarre, the flamboyant, the drugged and the drunk – if it's excessive, it's here. On weekends tourists and Sydney suburbanites flock to the Cross to glimpse a bit of weirdness.

The Cross's main drag is **Darlinghurst Road**; bohemian verging on sleazy, it's dotted with a jumble of bars, strip joints, fast-food outlets, tattoo parlours and X-rated book and video shops. But change is in the air as gentrification rapidly gains pace. Several strip clubs have shut down, and many brothels have moved to the suburbs. A number of trendy bars, cool nightclubs and boutique hotels have opened. Even the Bourbon and Beefsteak Bar, which was once a gloriously tacky icon of the Cross, has been given a slick revamp and a change of name to The Bourbon.

Old house in Kings Cross

In the evenings, you're likely to encounter prostitutes plying their trade from doorways in the Cross. Prostitution is legal in Sydney, provided streetwalkers observe rules such as staying away from schools, churches and private homes. The Cross has a thriving drug trade, which has survived all attempts to eradicate it, but you probably won't be offered drugs unless you seek them.

A 5-minute walk from Kings Cross train station, in Onslow Avenue, **Elizabeth Bay House** is a magnificent home built between 1835 and 1839 for the colonial secretary in the style of a Grecian villa. It serves as a reminder that Kings Cross was a fashionable address for at least a century. In the years after World War II, wealthier residents departed and less reputable elements moved in. Many former grand homes in the Cross were converted to boarding houses or backpacker lodgings.

The magnificent staircase at Elizabeth Bay House

Billyard Avenue runs in front of Elizabeth Bay House. If you follow this road downhill a short distance, past mansions hiding behind high walls, and turn left into Ithaca Road, you will come to a small waterfront park, which has lovely harbour views.

Balcony ironwork, Potts Point

Victoria Street, which runs off Darlinghurst Road, is a quieter alternative to the main strip. It's lined with gracious old homes, trendy cafés, such as Ulivetto, and fine restaurants, such as Mezzaluna. In the 1970s, Victoria Street became a battleground, with residents and unions pitted against rapacious property developers – the latter seeking to demolish homes to build high-rises. Juanita Nielsen, a celebrated Sydney heiress who edited a newspaper called *Now*, was a valiant campaigner for preservation. Although her efforts helped avert much high-rise ugliness, Ms Nielsen roused the ire of unscrupulous developers. She disappeared in July 1975 and was never seen again.

Also worth a look is Macleay Street, which runs through the upmarket residential area of **Potts Point**. Art Deco apartment buildings jostle with cafés, restaurants, bookshops, delis and art galleries, and there are occasional glimpses of the harbour.

Paddington

Another inner-city suburb worth investigating is Paddington, to the southeast of Kings Cross. Intricate wrought-ironwork, commonly known as Sydney Lace, is the local trademark; it adorns the balconies of many 19th-century terraced houses.

Paddington was developed for workers' housing in the 1880s, but fell into dilapidation and by the 1940s had become a slum. A slow process of gentrification then began, and by the 1970s 'Paddo', as the locals call it, had become a fashionable, rather artsy place to live.

The suburb is now fully gentrified, with residents more likely to be lawyers or stockbrokers than artists. The adjoining suburb of Woollahra, studded with mansions and consulates, is even more leafy and patrician, with an excellent set of shops down Queen Street and Jersey Road.

Paddington offers plenty of ethnic restaurants, antiques shops, art galleries, fashionable bookshops and trendy boutiques. One of Sydney's best public markets, Paddington Bazaar, is held each Saturday on the grounds of Paddington Public School on Oxford Street. It offers every type of art and craft and is enlivened by street entertainers.

Victorian shopfronts on Oxford Street

Oxford Street, particularly the section closest to the city centre, running through the suburb of Darlinghurst, is a centre for Sydney's large gay community. The Oxford Hotel (134 Oxford Street) is the street's longest-established gay pub, and there are many bars and nightclubs.

In Paddington proper is **Juniper Hall** (250 Oxford Street), Australia's oldest surviving example of a Georgian villa. Completed in 1824, it was built by the convict settler Robert Cooper, described as a 'distiller, publican and self-confessed smuggler', who lived there with his third wife, Sarah, and their children. Formerly concealed by a row of 1930s shops, Juniper Hall fell into disrepair until it was bought in 1984 by the National Trust of Australia and restored. The undistinguished row of shops was demolished while Juniper Hall survived. Next to Juniper Hall, Underwood Street leads to Heeley Street, a pleasant downhill walk that emerges 10 minutes later into Five Ways, with its pubs, shops and galleries.

Oxford Street is home to two of Sydney's best bookshops, Ariel and Berkelouw, and three of its more imaginative cinemas, the Chauvel, the Verona and the Academy Twin.

Victoria Barracks, built by convicts to house a regiment of British soldiers and their families, is Oxford Street's renowned example of mid-19th-century military architecture.

Centennial Park

In 1811, the far-sighted Governor Macquarie set aside an area outside the city for public use, naming it Sydney Common. The Governor's original 405-hectare (1,000-acre) bequest has been much whittled away since, alas, but Centennial Park at the eastern end of Oxford Street south of Woollahra is a welcome remnant. Centennial Park has provided greenery and fresh air to city folk since 1888, when it was dedicated on the centenary of Australia's foundation to 'the enjoyment of the people of New South Wales forever'.

The park's 220 hectares (544 acres) of trees, lawns, duck ponds, rose gardens, bridle-paths and sports fields are visited by about 3 million people a year, who cycle, rollerblade, walk their dogs, feed birds, throw frisbees, fly kites, picnic and barbecue.

Centennial Park, and Lachlan Swamp within it, support large numbers of birds. Among the many distinctive species are long-beaked ibises, which look like something off the wall of an ancient Egyptian tomb but are in fact native to Australia. Flocks of loud-squawking, sulphur-crested cockatoos regularly make their presence known. Bats twitter in the park's huge and venerable Moreton Bay fig trees, and possums (the native Australian type) dwell among the date palms. The palms themselves are under threat from a mysterious virus and are being progressively replaced with more resistant species.

Sydney Cricket Ground and Sydney Football Stadium

If you fancy a ride on the bridle path, check with Moore Park Stables (tel: 02 9360-8747). Bicycles and pedal-carts can be rented from Centennial Park Cycles (tel: 02 9398-5027).

Centennial Park Kiosk is a lovely setting for a meal and a glass of wine. Beside it stands a charming, if curious, modern stone fountain, incorporating an illuminated crystal that changes colour at night. Another park ornament, Federation Pavilion, is a ponderous, round, pillared structure with a bronze roof. Built in 1988 as part of the Bicentennial celebrations, it is inscribed with the motto: 'Mammon or Millennial Eden', a poet's question about which direction Australia is headed.

Not far from the Pavilion, Centennial Park Amphitheatre provides an outdoor venue for events and productions. In the summer months, a popular Moonlight Cinema programme is held in the amphitheatre. Films start at about 8.30pm and tickets are available at the gate from 7pm or in advance by booking online at www.moonlight.com.au.

Adjoining Centennial Park, Moore Park houses the **Sydney Cricket Ground** (a landmark to cricket fans around the world; Aussie Rules football is played here in winter), **Sydney Football Stadium** (for rugby league, rugby union and soccer) and the Equestrian Centre.

In a contentious move, 2 hectares (5 acres) of Moore Park were requisitioned for the Eastern Distributor Tollway through inner Sydney. More controversy followed when another 24 hectares (59 acres) of the park were handed over to US media tycoon Rupert Murdoch's Fox Group, for redevelopment into a studio and entertainment complex. The **Entertainment Quarter** (formerly Fox Studios) occupies the former Royal Agricultural Society Showground, where the Royal Easter Show was held for decades, before being moved to a new site next to Sydney Olympic Park at Homebush. As well as a 12-screen cinema complex, there are shops, bars, restaurants and cafés, an indoor children's playground, thrill rides, and live venues, such as the Comedy Store. A farmer's market takes place here every Wednesday and Saturday (10am–3.30pm), with a fashion and crafts market (Bent Street Bazaar) taking over every Sunday (10am–4pm).

INNER WEST SUBURBS

Newtown

Newtown, in Sydney's Inner West, 4km (2½ miles) from the CBD, is today's version of what Paddington was in the 1960s. Newtown's cosmopolitan nature and its high proportion of students (many attending the University of Sydney, just down the road) give the suburb a raffish flavour. Originally, Newtown consisted of farms on the outskirts of Sydney. Wealthy merchants built villas here in the early 1800s, but the late 19th century brought industry and workers' cottages and terraces. By the 1970s, Newtown had become a cheap-rent suburb.

Today, students, hippies, gays, lesbians, black-clad goths, New-Age traders and young families share the district, which has developed into a lively and entertaining quarter of delis, cafés, bookshops, second-hand clothing and retro-fashion outlets, pubs and multicultural restaurants, many of them offering excellent value.

Retail outlets on King Street, the suburb's main road, tend to be small-scale, typified by All Buttons Great and Small, which sells just that – buttons. The locale around the northern end of King Street has moved upmarket but gentrification has been contained, so far.

There are several bookshops, the longest-established being Gould's Book Arcade at 32 King Street, a huge emporium chock full of second-hand books. The shelving system is a bit haphazard there, but you can come up with surprising bargains if you are prepared to 'fossick' (an Australian term for search). The Dendy at 261 King Street shows art-house movies. The southern end of King Street takes on a Pacific Island flavour at weekends, when Sydney's Polynesian and Melanesian population heads there to shop for Pacific Island spices and produce.

Stallholders at the Saturday Market in Balmain

Newtown has some great pubs and bars including Kuletos at 157 King Street and Buzzbar at 349 King Street. The Bank Hotel 324 King Street is favoured by lesbians, while the Imperial Hotel (in neighbouring Erskineville) is a gay pub.

Balmain

Balmain, which is close to the CBD and easily accessible by ferry (from Wharf 5 at Circular Quay to Darling Street Wharf) and by bus (from the QVB or Central Station), is located on a peninsula and retains a sense of separateness from the city. A visit here by ferry, which sails beneath the Harbour Bridge, is strongly recommended.

Well into the latter half of the 20th century, Balmain was staunchly working class. The suburb was settled by sailors and boat-builders in the 1840s, and pubs have always been popular. In the 1880s there were 41 taverns in Balmain; now there are about 20. Balmain has become the abode of successful actors, lawyers, and others who can afford the steep property prices. Its village character survives, however.

Balmain's main street is Darling Street, where the trendy London Tavern stands more-or-less opposite St Andrews Congregational Church. A lively flea market takes place around the church on Saturdays, with all sorts of ethnic food stalls (Egyptian, Indian, Lebanese, vegetarian and others) arranged in the church hall and rows of stalls outside selling arts, crafts and second-hand goods. Often a band will entertain – a Romanian Gypsy trio, for instance.

You can walk virtually anywhere in Balmain and come across something interesting. Sydney Ferries publishes a harbour walks guide which includes directions for a memorable walk from Darling Street Wharf, along part of Darling Street, and into the neighbouring suburb of Birchgrove, ending at Birchgrove Wharf. You will pass pubs, neat little terrace houses, sandstone cottages dating from the early 19th century, quaint shops, cafés, restaurants and renovated warehouses. Louisa Road in Birchgrove is one of Sydney's top real-estate strips, with no shortage of millionaires' townhouses. There are great harbour views from Birchgrove Wharf.

Leichhardt

Not far from Newtown, the suburb of Leichhardt has been a base for Sydney's Italian community since the 19th century. First it hosted just a few Italian groceries. By 1962, four Italian cafés had sprung up, and other Italian stores followed. Fewer than 5 percent of Leichhardt's current population was born in Italy, but many residents of Italian extraction live in the suburb, which retains a strong Italian flavour. Norton Street is the best place to browse; eateries include Mezzapica, Bar Italia, Bar Sport and Osvaldo Polletti. The neighbouring suburb of Haberfield also has a very strong Italian flavour, and is home to some excellent pizzerias and Italian restaurants.

WESTERN SUBURBS

Sydney's western suburbs stretch for many kilometres, almost to the foot of the Blue Mountains. This is where the majority of Sydneysiders live. The visitor, however, can safely ignore most of it.

Parramatta

Parramatta, on the Parramatta River, is almost as old as Sydney. In the 1790s, many of Sydney's administrative functions and all its farming efforts were moved upriver to Parramatta, where the soil was more fertile. Governor Phillip said he would have founded the colony in this spot if he had known about it earlier. In 1804, a group of 260 Irish convicts led a rebellion at Parramatta aimed at overthrowing the governor, but troops crushed the uprising. Most of the conspirators were hanged.

Waterfront mansions on the Parramatta River

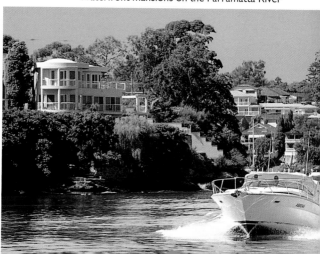

Many Parramatta buildings are new and not particularly inspiring, but a few places of interest remain, including Elizabeth Farm, Old Government House in Parramatta Park, and Experiment Farm cottage. For the most pleasant, and most scenic ride to Parramatta, catch one of the RiverCat catamaran ferries at Circular Quay.

Sydney Olympic Park

The Olympic Games last just two weeks but their effects linger. In Sydney's case, the 2000 Olympics created huge new parks and state-of-the-art sports facilities. The main site of the Games, **Sydney Olympic Park** is in the western suburb of Homebush.

The fastest way to get there is to take a train from Central Station to Olympic Park station. A more scenic alternative is to climb aboard a RiverCat (public catamaran ferry) at Circular Quay and cruise up the Parramatta River to Sydney Olympic Park wharf.

The visitor centre (tel: 02 9714-7888) has details of the range of tours available. You can pick up a map and do a self-

VIP Frogs Rule

The rare green and golden bell frog, a threatened species, makes its home in a disused brick-pit on part of the Sydney Olympic Park site. This reclusive little amphibian happens to bear Australia's sporting colours. Under the original Olympic site plan, the frog's home was to have been given way to the Olympic Tennis Centre. But the 300 or so frogs refused to move, even when a new pond was built for them. As a result, the Tennis Centre was moved and the brick-pit was incorporated into the area's parklands. The brick-pit is now used to store water for the Olympic site's recycled water system – a compromise that won't harm the frogs.

guided tour. Alternatively, an hour-long guided walking tour, the Games Trail, visits the various sporting facilities and also includes entry to the observation deck of the Novotel Olympic Park, which gives panoramic views of the Olympic site, the Blue Mountains, the Harbour Bridge and the city's skyscrapers. There are also tours of the site's largest facilities, ANZ Stadium and the Sydney International Aquatic Centre, as well as nature-orientated tours of the area's

A wallaby with a joey at
Featherdale Wildlife Park

wetlands. You can hire a bike to explore the large parkland area that surrounds Sydney Olympic Park.

Featherdale Wildlife Park

Those interested in getting close to normally shy Australian wildlife should make the trip to **Featherdale Wildlife Park** (daily 9am–5pm; charge; www.featherdale.com.au) in the suburb of Doonside, about an hour's drive from the CBD. You can feed the kangaroos and wallabies, get your photo taken with a koala, watch the crocodiles being fed, or just wander around admiring the other animal inmates, including wombats, emus, dingoes, Tasmanian devils, snakes and a variety of birdlife. The park can be reached by taking a train from the city to Blacktown and then a bus to the park entrance; some bus tours also stop at the park on their way to the Blue Mountains. The park is a past winner of a New South Wales tourism award.

Bondi is Sydney's most popular beach

THE BEACHES

Sydney has dozens of beaches, offering everything from raging surf to lapping waves. At ocean beaches heed the advice to swim only between the red-and-yellow flags, which indicate sections of beach patrolled by professional lifeguards or volunteer lifesavers. Strong currents and tidal rips are a feature of many Sydney beaches; drownings are an unfortunate part of every summer – many victims are tourists who swim outside the flags or are unused to swimming in strong surf. Drowning between the flags, however, is virtually unheard of.

▶ Bondi Beach

Pronounced 'bond-eye', Australia's most famous stretch of sand is central Sydney's nearest beach, easily accessible by bus Nos 380 or 382 from Circular Quay or by train to Bondi Junction, from where there are frequent buses to the beach.

Site of surf shops, cafés and lively alfresco restaurants, Bondi has been popular ever since trams started running there in 1894. Its appeal has outlasted the trams. Style purists consider Bondi's appearance a bit tacky, but its fortunes are climbing and the suburb has become quite fashionable. Many Australian celebrities call Bondi home. Bondi Pavilion, which houses dressing rooms for 5,000 people, a grand ballroom and other vital beach facilities, displays photos of the beach dating back to the mid-19th century, when it was privately owned and utterly deserted.

Backpackers use Bondi to celebrate Christmas riotously and see in the New Year. Mainstream beach-users include lithe and leathery veteran sun-worshippers, fanatical surfers and families at play. Bondi is Sydney's most popular beach and it can be crowded, especially on weekends.

The cliffs around Bondi's southern end offer a bracing walk and enchanting views, especially in the early evening by the light of a full moon. If you follow the walk south from Bondi, you will reach **Tamarama Beach**, popular with the body-beautiful set. Next stop is **Bronte Beach**, backed by palms and pines. It has great facilities, including a sea pool for those who dislike strong surf, and a big park for picnicking. Further along are **Clovelly Beach**, basically a very large and sheltered rock pool, and then the much larger **Coogee Beach**. Popular with backpackers, it usually has gentle surf, making it good for swimming.

Literary cemetery

Just after Bronte Beach, the walk from Bondi to Coogee passes through Waverley Cemetery, overlooking the ocean. Two of Australia's best-known poets are buried here. Dorothea Mackellar (1885–1968) wrote *My Country*, whose lines are still memorised by Australian schoolchildren. Henry Lawson (1867–1922) wrote bush ballads and humorous short stories.

Vaucluse and South Head

The peninsula jutting north from Bondi to Watsons Bay and culminating in South Head offers superlative beaches and great walks. Sydney's most expensive residential real estate is located around here, in Vaucluse (just south of Watsons Bay), and in Point Piper (a peninsula to the west of Vaucluse, separated from it by the almost equally wealthy suburb of Rose Bay).

The Bondi Explorer bus *(see page 123)* allows you to travel on a scenic tour from Circular Quay to Watsons Bay, where you can get out and admire Pacific Ocean views from the Gap, a dramatic seafront cliff and notorious suicide leap. Alternatively, take the ferry from Circular Quay to Watsons

Sydney's Nudist Beaches

Sydney has three legally sanctioned nudist beaches. The most accessible is Lady Bay, also known as Lady Jane Bay, near Watsons Bay, just around the bend from Camp Cove. The other nude venues are Cobblers Beach and Obelisk Beach. The first is east of the North Shore's Balmoral Beach; the second is located near Georges Heights, Mosman. Access to Cobblers is easy by boat but difficult by land.

Dress on Sydney's beaches has come a long way over the past century. In the 1900s, the law permitted public swimming only in the early morning and after dark. This law was successfully challenged, and by the 1920s the beaches of Sydney were crowded with people, but they had to wear neck-to-knee bathing costumes. In 1935, an ordinance was passed forbidding men to wear swimming attire that exposed their chests. Beach inspectors were empowered to remove offenders to a dressing enclosure, where they could be compelled to clothe themselves 'respectably'. By the 1960s, regulations had mellowed considerably, although beach inspectors still prowled the sands searching for excessively brief costumes (the focus by that time had shifted to women).

Bay Wharf. Houses in the Vaucluse/Watsons Bay area are lavish but tasteful, with occasional exceptions to each of those criteria. The winding streets are bougainvillea-lined, and the surroundings have a secluded, villagey charm. All along the route you'll catch splendid views of the city.

Camp Cove at **Watsons Bay** is the spot where Governor Arthur Phillip first stepped ashore in Sydney Harbour (on 20 January 1788) after abandoning Botany Bay further south. The governor had taste – the beach at Camp Cove is one of Sydney's finest. A plaque

Sailing below Vaucluse

notes where Phillip landed. For a short but very worthwhile excursion, take the stairs at the northern end of the beach (to your right as you face the harbour) and follow the path to South Head lighthouse, which stands on a headland overlooking the entrance to Sydney Harbour. The views of harbour and ocean are magnificent. Also at Watsons Bay is the very popular Doyles on the Beach, a near-legendary – and expensive – seafood restaurant.

Vaucluse House, a stately home with its own beach in the pretty suburb of Vaucluse, adds its mock-Gothic turrets to Sydney's harbour skyline. The mansion began as the home of a colourful convict, Sir Henry Brown Hayes, the Sheriff of Cork before he was banished to Australia for the abduction of his bride. In the 1830s the new owner, William Wentworth, expanded it into a 15-room homestead. The grounds are open daily 10am–5pm and the house is open Fri, Sat and Sun 9.30am–4.30pm; admission fee for house.

Not far south of Watsons Bay (towards the city) is **Nielsen Park**, full of shady trees and one of Sydney's top spots for picnicking and swimming. It is part of Sydney Harbour National Park. Nielsen Park has its own excellent little bay – which is generally referred to as Nielsen Park Bay rather than its real name, Shark Bay. The beach is shark-netted (netting was introduced in the 1930s), so you needn't fear any risk of being nipped. If you feel like tucking into some food, a kiosk serves snacks and good espresso. The headland towards Vaucluse Point (to the right of the beach when you face the harbour) is often quite secluded, even on public holidays. To the left of the beach, a walking track takes you southwards along the harbour's edge almost to Rose Bay.

Manly

Manly is reached from Circular Quay by ferry or high-speed JetCat catamaran across Sydney Harbour. The JetCats are quicker (20 minutes), but the ferry (30 minutes) is more relaxing. Manly offers a choice of two beaches – one open to the ocean and popular with surfers, the other a calm harbourside crescent suitable for children – and excellent views of Sydney Harbour. The area was named by Governor Phillip, who thought the Aborigines sunning themselves on the beach had a commanding ('manly') presence.

Linking the two beaches, the Corso is a promenade, lined with shops, cafés, restaurants and fast-food emporia; fish 'n' chips is a speciality. Manly maintains a holiday atmosphere and has for decades used the slogan, 'Seven miles from Sydney – and a thousand miles from care.'

Manly has a relaxed holiday atmosphere

The oceanside beach, divided into North Steyne and South Steyne, is lined with Norfolk pines and pleasant cafés. If you walk south (to the right as you face the ocean) along South Steyne, you end up at Shelly Beach Park, with a sheltered little beach perfect for children. The park is a romantic place at sunset, when the sky turns red and gold.

Although not as impressive as Sydney Aquarium, **Ocean-world Manly** (to the left of the ferry terminal as you arrive; open daily 10am–5.30pm; charge) makes a good outing for children. Divers hand-feed sharks and giant stingrays every day – an awesome spectacle. Oceanworld Manly denizens include colourful Great Barrier Reef fish and a giant cuttlefish with three hearts and green blood. A moving walkway traverses an acrylic tunnel surrounded by freely swimming sharks, rays, and their friends. Oceanworld also displays a range of lizards, young crocodiles and poisonous Australian snakes.

A path runs from Manly to the Spit Bridge, a distance of almost 10km (6 miles), or 4 hours' walking time. The route stays close to the harbour all the way, and features bushland, beaches and bays, as well as harbour views. There are opportunities for swims and refreshments along the way, and at Grotto Point there are Aboriginal rock carvings.

Northern Beaches

North of Manly, a couple of Pacific beaches with charming names, **Curl Curl** and **Dee Why**, offer good surfing. **Collaroy** and **Narrabeen** are linked by a single beach with an ocean pool, ideal for families. **Newport Beach** is a beautiful, broad sweep of sand. **Avalon Beach** is known for surfing and popular with children. **Whale Beach** is another good surfing beach with a wonderfully relaxed feel to it. At the northern tip of the Sydney beach region, **Palm Beach** – the abode of millionaires, actors (the soap opera *Home and Away* is filmed here) and advertising types – is in a class of its own. Manicured, nicely gardened villas occupy the hills of the peninsula behind the beach. If you're feeling like a climb, you can walk to the top of Barrenjoey Point at the beach's northern end. From the base of the lighthouse there are fantastic views over the mouth of Broken Bay – which marks Sydney's northern boundary – with Lion Island below you and more beaches stretching away on the other side. You can get to Palm Beach by taking the 190 bus from outside Wynyard railway station in the city.

A young surfer on Palm Beach

The Three Sisters rock formation in the Blue Mountains

EXCURSIONS FROM SYDNEY

Within striking distance of Sydney – by car, train or sight-seeing coach – a choice of scene-changers shows the wide variety of attractions on offer in New South Wales. Any of the more popular outings will deepen your understanding of Australia and its assets.

Blue Mountains

Undeveloped native forest protected within national parks surrounds Sydney on three sides. The most popular destination – 1½-hours' drive or a 2-hour rail trip west of the city – is **Blue Mountains National Park**, one of the most spectacular and captivating wilderness areas in Australia. The mountains really do look blue, given the right conditions: the blue tint is created by the refraction of light through the haze of volatile eucalyptus oil evaporating from the trees.

You can sign up for one of the many day tours from Sydney, or you can visit and explore at your own pace. Don't expect sharp peaks such as those in the Swiss Alps or Wyoming's Grand Tetons – the range is far too ancient and eroded for that. Here, immense, bush-filled canyons and ravines, weathered precipices, deep river valleys and soaring sandstone cliffs awe the viewer. The main road through the mountains is the Great Western Highway, which begins its climb through a succession of towns, with the forest yawning below and lines of hills gradually dissolving into the pale-blue eucalyptus haze.

Rising to a height of more than 1,300m (4,260ft), the Blue Mountains offer crisp air, vast sandstone valleys where waterfalls shatter on the rocks, gardens that burn with autumn colour, English-style homesteads and little towns of wood and stone. Several grand, old-style hotels (including the

Katoomba Cascades, one of many waterfalls in the national park

sprawling, Art Deco Hydro Majestic Hotel, at Medlow Bath, built as a European-style spa in the 1930s) complement historic towns, including Katoomba, Black-heath, Wentworth Falls, Leura and Mount Victoria.

A day's drive takes in the major attractions. The **City of the Blue Mountains** (comprising 26 towns and villages) is one of the few places in Australia cold enough to snow (occasion-

Jurassic plant

The Wollemi pine, the world's oldest species of tree, was discovered in a remote part of the Blue Mountains in 1994. The tree's closest relations became extinct during the Jurassic and Cretaceous periods – 65–200 million years ago. As one Sydney-based botanist exclaimed at the time, 'This is like finding a living dinosaur in your backyard.'

ally) in mid-winter, usually around August. At that time, one of the Blue Mountains' most photographed rugged sandstone formations, the **Three Sisters**, is sometimes dusted with snow. Local guesthouses stage 'Yulefests' in the winter (July), complete with Santa Claus and traditional Christmas fare.

The Blue Mountains' largest town, **Katoomba**, is the usual starting point for most visitors. Nearby **Echo Point** has viewing platforms that give breathtaking views of the national park's forested valleys and near-vertical sandstone cliffs. A number of walking tracks start from here, suitable for walkers of all fitness levels; information on them is avail-able from Echo Point's visitor information centre.

If you have the energy, descend the Giant Stairway and walk down into the Jamison Valley, then take the **Scenic Railway** back up. The railway is a 3-minute hair-raising ride along an old mining cart track with the steepest incline in the world. The clifftop railway terminus is at **Scenic World** (daily 9am–5pm), a tourist complex a short distance to the west of Echo Point. Scenic World also offers two other thrilling experiences: the **Scenic Cableway**, which descends over 500m (1,600ft) into the Jamison Valley, and the **Scenic Skyway**, a cable car dangling high above the valley.

If you have time to spare, take a trip to a less touristed lookout, **Govetts Leap**, near Blackheath, 12km (7½ miles) west of Katoomba. The views are perhaps even more spectacular, while the comparative lack of crowds gives a better sense of the wilderness around you.

Jenolan Caves

Further along the Great Western Highway, about 60km (38 miles) from Mount Victoria, is Australia's most famous underground attraction. Explorers have yet to penetrate the entire labyrinth of Jenolan Caves, but thousands have admired the stalactites and stalagmites of the nine caves open to the public. Guided tours through the spooky but often awesome limestone caverns last about an hour and a half.

Hunter Valley

The best-known wine-growing region in New South Wales is the Hunter Valley, a 2-hour drive north of Sydney. You can visit it as a day trip, but it's also a very popular destination for weekenders. It is possible to drive there independently, but a better option is to join a organised wine-tasting tour from Sydney.

Wine making is nothing new to this region. Vines from France and Spain were transplanted here early in the life of the colony, and by the mid-19th century, the region was producing hundreds of thousands of bottles of wine a year. More recent refinements to the production process have resulted in a number of high-quality vintages.

The towns of **Cessnock** and **Pokolbin** are the main centres of the Lower Hunter Valley wine region. The visitor centre at Pokolbin supplies touring maps and brochures (tel: 02 4990-0900). The Hunter's 60 or so wineries harvest their grapes in

Vineyard in the Hunter Valley

February and March, but they welcome visitors throughout the year. With its neat, rolling vineyards, the Lower Hunter is one of Australia's most attractive wine-producing regions.

Most of the Hunter wineries are open for tastings. Major wineries include Tyrell's Wines, Lindemans Winery, Wyndham Estate, the Rosemount Estate, Rothbury Estate and the McWilliams Estate. The wines made by big-name producers shouldn't lull you into neglecting 'boutique' wines, many of which can be obtained only by buying a bottle from the person who tended the vines, picked the grapes and fretted over fermentation. The wineries are at their best on a warm summer evening, when the breeze blows through the vines.

When not in the vineyards, visitors to the Hunter Valley can amuse themselves with horse riding, cycling, bushwalking, golf, tennis, water sports and hot-air ballooning. If you're feeling whimsical, try a picnic on a horse-drawn carriage or a bicycle trip along the vine trail.

Hawkesbury River

The Hawkesbury River winds for 480km (about 300 miles) on its way to the Pacific at Broken Bay, just beyond Palm Beach in the most northerly section of Greater Sydney. The Hawkesbury's gentle waters and ever-changing vistas – coves and bays and steep wooded banks – delight visitors. There's no need to own a boat; there are many places where you can hire one – Brooklyn, an hour's drive from Sydney is one, so is Akuna Bay in Ku-ring-gai Chase National Park (a 40-minute drive from Sydney). Try, for example, Holidays Afloat (tel: 02 9985-7368) at Brooklyn, which rents out houseboats that can sleep from two to ten people, or Akuna Bay's Clipper Cruiser Holidays (tel: 02 9450-0000), which offers 34-ft (10.4-m) cruisers sleeping between two and eight people each. You don't need a licence or any boating experience. Once you have your vessel, you can spend the day fishing, go ashore to find your own little beach, follow a trail through the national park, or just lie back on the deck and enjoy a good book.

Ku-ring-gai Chase National Park covers 15,000 hectares (37,000 acres) of bushland fringing the Hawkesbury. If the idea of boating doesn't appeal, there are a number of scenic walks in the park, some leading down to secluded coves and beaches where, on weekdays, you may well be the only visitor. The Resolute Track leads to Aboriginal rock-art sites. West Head, within the park, has panoramic views of the Hawkesbury, Broken Bay, Pittwater (a bay to the west of Palm Beach) and the coast to the north. Park information is available from the Bobbin Head Visitor Centre, tel: 02 9472-8949.

The Hawkesbury area might have become Australia's national capital. In 1899, an extraordinary, utopian plan arose to build an Australian capital on the Hawkesbury headlands. To be called Pacivica, the city would have included buildings modelled on the Tower of London, Windsor Castle and other architectural icons of the Empire. (The only thing missing was the Taj Mahal.) As you cruise these secluded waterways, you'll be delighted the plan was set aside.

Southern Highlands

Lush grazing land and orchards dotted with historic towns and villages lie to the southwest of Sydney. Towns worth visiting include picturesque **Mittagong** and **Bowral**, a prettily gardened town that holds a tulip festival every October. Charming **Berrima** is a Georgian gem so well preserved the whole town is listed as a national monument. There are plenty of antiques shops, arts-and-crafts galleries and atmospheric tearooms. Among the most distinguished monuments, the Surveyor General Inn, established in 1834, claims to be Australia's oldest continuously licensed inn. It makes an appealing spot for a drink or a meal. Another landmark, Berrima Gaol, was built in the 1830s by those who were soon to inhabit it.

A misty morning in the Southern Highlands

Canberra

Canberra, Australia's custom-built national capital, lies about 300km (185 miles) southwest of Sydney at the heart of the Australian Capital Territory, a 240-sq-km (93-sq-mile) expanse of farmland, mountains, forests and valleys. If you plan to visit Canberra from Sydney as a day trip, you are better off flying. Flights are frequent and take just 40 minutes. Buses make the journey daily, but the trip lasts over 3 hours each way. There are also three trains a day from Sydney.

Many visitors to Australia relegate Canberra to a day trip, only to realise after arrival the city is worth much more. Canberra boasts some of Australia's finest galleries and public buildings, and perhaps the loveliest surroundings of any national capital. Sydneysiders tend to look askance at Canberra, because of the high proportion of politicians and civil servants who live there. But although Canberra's streets are

Parliament House

curiously devoid of pedestrians compared to other Australian cities, there is much to commend the capital.

Created in 1901 when Australia decided it needed an independent capital free from political or commercial domination by any one state, Canberra was designed by the Chicago landscape architect Walter Burley Griffin.

Seeing Canberra

There are several good ways to see Canberra – but not on foot. The distances are greater than you think. If you do want to walk, many of the main attractions are found near Lake Burley Griffin. It's a good idea to sign up for a bus tour; they come in half-day and all-day versions.

A planned community created straight from the blueprints, Canberra has no old quarter and few restored historic buildings. The city's most prominent structure, **Parliament House** (daily 9am–5pm; free) on Capital Hill, opened in 1988. It replaced an earlier building from 1927, which now houses the **National Portrait Gallery** (daily 9am–5pm; charge). Other attractions include the Australian National University, the National Film and Sound Archives, the Australian Institute of Sport, the National Museum of Australia and the National Science and Technology Centre.

More than 30 artistic and cultural institutions are located in Canberra, ranging from Questacon (a hands-on facility at the National Science and Technology Centre) to the **National Gallery of Australia** (daily 10am–5pm; free) on the banks of Lake Burley Griffin. The gallery houses the most extensive collection in Australia – highlights range from Aboriginal masterpieces and Australian painter Sidney Nolan's *Ned Kelly* series to Monet's *Water Lilies* and Jackson Pollock's *Blue Poles*. Another major cultural institution, the **Australian War Memorial** (daily 10am–5pm; free), is an excellent museum devoted to Australian military history. The capital's other diversions include clubs, music venues and restaurants.

WHAT TO DO

SHOPPING

Sydney shopping hours generally run from 9am to 5.30pm, Monday to Friday, 9am to 5pm on Saturday, and 9am–4pm on Sunday. Shops do not close for lunch. Thursday is late shopping night in the Central Business District (CBD), when many stores stay open until 9pm. Other suburban centres have late-night shopping on other nights. Some shops at Darling Harbour and The Rocks stay open until 9pm daily.

Acceptance of American Express, Visa and MasterCard credit cards is virtually universal in Sydney, with lesser-known cards accepted at larger enterprises. International travellers can buy goods duty-free, by producing their air ticket and passport at the duty-free store when making a purchase. On departure the goods must be shown to the customs agent, who is tipped off by a computer system. (For further information on duty-free allowances, *see page 112*.)

Where to Shop

In central Sydney, skyscrapers sit above subterranean shopping arcades. **Pitt Street Mall** is a pedestrian-only street linked to several shopping plazas. For shopping in a historic atmosphere, try the **Queen Victoria Building (QVB)** on George Street, or the stylish **Strand Arcade**, a Victorian masterpiece running between George and Pitt

The historic Strand Arcade

Tax refunds

Australia operates a Tourist Refund Scheme under which overseas visitors can claim a refund of the 10 percent Goods and Services Tax (GST) added to most purchases. See *page 124* for details of how to claim.

streets. Some of Australia's leading fashion designers have boutiques on the upper levels of the Strand. It's also worth inspecting the jewellery shops here. Other shopping locations include the **Imperial Arcade**, running between Pitt and Castlereagh streets, the adjacent **Skygarden** and **Centrepoint**, **Glasshouse** on King Street, and **Galeries Victoria** on George Street opposite the QVB. The local outlets for such upmarket international brands as Gucci and Louis Vuitton are clustered in and around the **MLC Centre**, while **Chifley Square** is home to several local and international fashion labels. Go to Darlinghurst, Paddington or Woollahra for local jewellery and fashion designers. Sydney's main department stores are David Jones (on Market Street) and Myer (on Pitt Street Mall).

What to Buy

Aboriginal art. Aboriginal artists sell their work in art centres, specialist galleries and craft retailers and through agents. Each artist owns the rights to his or her particular stories, motifs and totems. Fabric designs by artists such as Jimmy Pike are eagerly sought. The Outback Centre or Gavala Aboriginal Art Centre, both at Darling Harbour, are good places to start.

Avoiding fakes

Fakes and kitsch are sometimes represented as Aboriginal art by unscrupulous traders. To help identify genuine Aboriginal and Torres Strait Islander art, Aboriginal communities have developed the Label of Authenticity, which employs the Aboriginal colours black, red and yellow and is protected by law.

Antiques. The Paddington and Woollahra district is full of antiques shops. Worthy pieces to seek out include clocks, jewellery, porcelain, silverware, glassware, books and maps.

Fashion. Sydney's end-of-season sales are ideal for visitors from the Northern Hemisphere. Just as a season is ending in Australia, the same one is about to begin

Authentic didgeridoos

north of the equator. Local labels include Country Road, Trent Nathan, Akira, Collette Dinnigan, Morrissey, Wayne Cooper, Scanlan & Theodore, Saba, and Marcs. For beachwear, look for the Billabong and Mambo labels. Specifically for women are the 'wearable art' of Ken Done and the swimwear of Zimmermann or Tigerlily.

Outback clothing. A distinct style of clothing has evolved in Australia's rural bush. Driza-bone oilskin raincoats, Akubra hats and the R.M. Williams range of bushwear (including boots and moleskin trousers) are good examples. Blundstone boots, known for their durability, are another. Australian merino sheep produce fine fleece ideally suited for spinning. All sorts of knitwear, from vivid children's clothing to greasy wool sweaters (which retain the sheep's natural water resistance), are available throughout the city.

Opals. Australia is the source of most of the world's opals. 'White' opals are mined from the fields of Andamooka

Fine opals on sale in Sydney

and Coober Pedy in South Australia. 'Boulder' opals – bright and vibrant – come from Quilpie in Queensland, while the precious 'black' opal is mined at Lightning Ridge and White Cliffs in New South Wales.

Sapphires. After opals, sapphires are Australia's most-mined gemstones. A sapphire is exactly the same stone as a ruby – the only difference is the name and the colour. Creative Australian jewellers work wonders with sapphires.

Diamonds. Australia has one of the world's richest deposits of diamonds. The gems are mined by Argyle Diamond Mines in the Kimberley region in the west. Kimberley is famed for its 'pink' diamonds, sometimes marketed under the description 'champagne'. Hues range from lightly flushed to deep red.

SPORTS

Too much sport is barely enough. That's the way Sydneysiders feel about their weekends. If not actually playing or watching sport, they are reading about it, arguing about it, listening to it on the radio, watching it on TV or betting on it.

Participatory Sports

Swimming and sunning. With dozens of alluring beaches and Olympic-size pools within easy reach, swimming is a major activity in Sydney. The more popular beaches are marked by yellow-and-red flags showing where it's safe to swim. Beware of strong undertows or shifting currents and obey the instructions of the lifeguards. If a shark alert is sounded (rare), beat a retreat to the shore. Other dangers are bluebottles, jellyfish-like creatures that inflict a painful (but non-fatal) sting. Blue-ringed octopuses are more dangerous but rare. Apply sunscreen to exposed skin, wear a hat, and try to stay out of the midday sun.

Surfing. Surfboard and bodyboard riders are not allowed within the swimming areas marked by yellow-and-red flags; 'surfcraft' areas are marked by signs. Bondi Beach is the best-known surfing zone in Australia. Manly is another favourite. Many surf schools offer lessons in board-riding – try Let's Go Surfing (at Bondi; tel: 02 9365-1800) or Manly Surf School (tel: 02 9977-6977). Surfing carnivals are among the highlights of the Sydney season, from November to March.

Catching a wave off Bondi

Scuba diving. North Head (near Manly) and Gordons Bay (near Bondi) are favourite spots for scuba divers. There are many other dive sites in New South Wales, though none is as spectacular as those of the Great Barrier Reef. For information on the scuba scene, contact the Australian Underwater Federation (www.auf.com.au).

Fishing. Rock fishing is a very popular Sydney pastime. The Sydney Game Fishing Club at Watsons Bay (www.sgfc.com.au) can provide information about deep-sea

Climbing the Harbour Bridge

expeditions from Sydney. The icy streams of the Snowy Mountains, near Canberra, are renowned for their out-standing trout fishing. Details from Tourism New South Wales (tel: 02 9931-1111).

Sailing. Sailing on Sydney Harbour is an unforgettable experience. You can rent a boat (from the Balmoral Boat Shed at Balmoral Beach, for example, tel: 02 9969-6006), or learn to sail (Sydney by Sail, tel: 02 9280-1110). There are also several good windsurfing locations, such as off Balmoral Beach, where you can rent boards (tel: 02 9960-5344).

Boating and Kayaking. Powerboats can be chartered, with or without a professional skipper. Inland, you can command a boat on the relaxing Hawkesbury River *(see page 78)*. Kayaking is a fun way to explore the harbour. Kayaks can be hired at several locations, including Balmoral Beach (tel: 02 9960- 5344), the Spit Bridge between Mosman and Manly (tel: 02 9960-4389) and near Manly wharf.

Tennis. You'll find no shortage of courts or partners in Sydney. Local councils run the courts and the fees are cheap.

Golf. Sydney is full of parks – closer inspection reveals that many are in fact golf courses. Golf is one of Australia's most popular participant sports, with about 400,000 players out of a population of about 20 million. Australian players like Greg Norman, Steve Elkington and Robert Allenby have boosted the game's popularity. The Australian Golf Club in Sydney was formed in 1882, and thousands of golfers exer-cise their skills each weekend at 115 courses and driving ranges throughout the city. Nearly half of these are public courses available for a casual game at reasonable rates. Moore Park Golf Course (tel: 02 9663-1064) is a pleasant venue a short cab ride of the CBD, and a number of picturesque courses are scattered throughout the North Shore. Many of the private clubs welcome visiting players, although a member's invitation may be necessary. Some of the more exclusive clubs have strict dress codes.

Spectator Sports

Rugby. Several types of rugby are popular. Rugby League is the main event in Sydney. It is a freeflowing game with 13-player teams and plently of crunching tackles. Rugby Union, with teams of 15, has more complex passages of play, with 8-man scrums and skillful passing. The main ground for both codes is Sydney Football Stadium, near Centennial Park. Aussie Rules Football combines elements of rugby and Gaelic

Walking Above Sydney

Two companies offer tours that require a good head for heights:

BridgeClimb (tel: 02 8274-7777; www.bridgeclimb.com) conducts guided walks for small groups over the massive arches of the Sydney Harbour Bridge. The walk is 1,500m (about a mile) long and reaches the top of the bridge, 150m (490ft) above sea level. Tickets cost from A$179, and climbers depart from 5 Cumberland Street, The Rocks.

Far above the Bridgeclimbers are the Skywalkers of Sydney Tower, 260m (850ft) above the city's streets. **Skywalk** (tel: 02 9333-9222; www.skywalk.com.au) advertises itself as 'an exhilarating outdoor walk on the roof of the city'. Participants are harnessed to walkways on the edge of the tower's turret, where they walk across a glass-floored viewing platform. The Skywalk office is located at Sydney Tower, Centrepoint Podium Level, 100 Market Street. Skywalk costs about $A65.

football, and is a comparative newcomer to Sydney. Look for long-distance kicks and passes and high scores on a large, circular field with 18 players a side. Sydney Cricket Ground (next to Sydney Football Stadium) hosts the big games.

Football. Football (soccer) is also played and is increasing in popularity. Sydney Football Stadium hosts some games.

Cricket. Cricket is an Australian passion, and the country has produced some of the world's greatest players. The traditional five-day Test matches draw thousands of fans to the Sydney Cricket Ground every summer. Games of one-day cricket and the recently introduced Twenty20 take less time to complete and the teams wear coloured kits.

Horse racing. The races in Sydney are a glorious spectacle. Sydney has four courses: Canterbury Park, Rosehill Gardens, Warwick Farm and Royal Randwick. The last is closest to the CBD. Races go on all year, on Wednesdays and Saturdays, and big carnivals are held in spring and autumn.

ENTERTAINMENT

The *Sydney Morning Herald* publishes a lift-out arts and music guide on Friday and an entertainment section on Saturday. Free weekly guides detailing alternative music and dance attractions are available at many inner-city pubs and bookshops.

Theatre. Sydney has a flourishing theatre scene covering mainstream and alternative productions. Big musicals and shows are staged at venues like the State Theatre (a former cinema decorated in over-the-top 1929 rococo-

Putting on a show

In 1789, just a year after New South Wales was founded, a troupe of convicts actors put on a Restoration comedy (*The Recruiting Officer*) by George Farquhar as part of the celebrations for the birthday of King George III.

Theatregoers on the foyer staircase at the Capitol Theatre

revival style) or the Capitol Theatre. The city's leading theatre group is the Sydney Theatre Company (tel: 02 9250-1777; www.sydneytheatre.com.au), which stages its plays mainly at the Wharf Theatre, the nearby Sydney Theatre and the Opera House Drama Theatre. Other major groups are the Belvoir Street Theatre (tel: 02 9699-3444; www.belvoir.com.au) at Surry Hills, the Ensemble Theatre Company (tel: 02 9929-0644; www.ensemble.com.au) at Kirribilli, and the Bell Shakespeare Company (tel: 02 8298-2700; www.bellshakespeare. com.au), at the Opera House Drama Theatre.

Opera. Opera Australia (tel: 02 9699-1099; www.opera-australia.org.au), based in Sydney, performs at the Sydney Opera House nine months of the year (January, February, and part of March, and from June to November).

Dance. The Australian Ballet (tel: 03 9669-2700; www. australianballet.com.au), founded in 1962, is headquartered in Melbourne but spends nearly half its time performing in

Sydney, at the Opera House. Sydney Dance Company (tel: 02 9221-4811; www.sydneydancecompany.com) is the city's foremost modern dance troupe. The Bangarra Dance Theatre (tel: 02 9251-5333; www.bangarra.com.au) is an Aboriginal group which performs in a variety of venues.

Concerts. The concert hall of the Sydney Opera House, City Recital Hall (www.cityrecitalhall.com) and the Conservatorium of Music (www.music.usyd.edu.au) are the main venues for classical music. The Opera House is home to Australia's leading orchestra, the Sydney Symphony (tel: 02 9334-4644; www.symphony.org.au).

Other live music. Jazz, blues and rock bands play at pubs and clubs all over the city. Popular venues include Selina's at Coogee Bay, the Metro on Geroge Street in the CBD, the Enmore Theatre in Newtown, The Factory in Marrickville, and, for big gigs, the Hordern Pavilion in Moore Park or

Bangarra Dance Theatre

the Sydney Entertainment Centre. The Basement in Reiby Place near Circular Quay is known for its jazz.

Cinema. In central Sydney, George Street south of the Town Hall has multi-screen cinema complexes that show popcorn movies. Less mainstream films are shown at the Dendy Opera Quays, at a great location near the Opera House, and in Paddington at the Academy Twin, the Verona and the Chauvel. In summer, two outdoor cinemas put Sydney's balmy evenings to good use: the Moonlight Cinema (www.moonlight.com.au), in Centennial Park's Amphitheatre, and the OpenAir Cinema (www.stgeorge.com.au/openair; tel: 1300-366-649) in the Royal Botanic Gardens facing the Opera House.

Mardi Gras

Sydney is one of the world's most hospitable cities for gay visitors. The best-known gay and lesbian event in Australia is the Sydney **Gay and Lesbian Mardi Gras Parade**, which takes place each February and attracts the largest crowds of any event in the country. The climactic finale of a month-long festival of gay art, culture, music, theatre and dance, the parade culminates in a wild party. Tickets to the party usually sell out before the end of January, but you don't need a ticket to watch the parade.

The prototype of the Mardi Gras parade was a protest march in 1978, held to commemorate the Stonewall riots in New York City. The Sydney march was broken up by police in no uncertain terms, a crackdown that produced the same effect as the infamous police raid on New York's Stonewall Inn. A wave of indignation and fury swept the gay community. A series of protests, with 178 arrests, led the New South Wales Government to repeal the Summary Offences Act, which had previously made street marches and acts of public affection between males illegal.

The parade now features about 100 floats and 5,000 participants and attracts tens of thousands of spectators. Regular paraders include Dykes on Bikes, the Marching Drags and the Sisters of Perpetual Indulgence (a group of bearded 'nuns'). There is truly something for everyone.

Sydney Festival

The **Sydney Festival** (www.sydneyfestival.org.au) happens in January. This multi-media happening aims to present a world of entertainment in three weeks of sensational theatre, dance, music, outdoor exhibitions and visual arts, culminating on Australia Day, 26 January. The Opera House is illuminated in a different festival theme colour each year. International opera stars, avant-garde theatre companies, open-air cinema, circuses and dancers join forces with local acts to entertain crowds at various venues. The Domain hosts large and popular open-air jazz or symphonic music concerts on Saturday nights.

New Year's Eve fireworks

The **Sydney Fringe Festival** runs alongside the main event. Its offerings tend to be small-scale, such as open-mic comedy events.

Nightlife

Sydney's nightlife is dazzling in its scope and variety. If you're looking for a relaxed evening out in a period setting **The Rocks** is the place to be. Try the historic Lord Nelson Brewery Hotel, 19 Kent Street, or the Hero of Waterloo, 81 Lower Fort, which claims to be Sydney's oldest pub. The Shangri-La Hotel's classy top-floor Blu Horizon Bar, 176 Cumberland Street, has sensational views of the harbour. A little further afield, **Bondi Beach** offers a seaside atmosphere and great views of the Pacific: Icebergs Dining Room and Bar and Hotel Bondi are both right on the beach.

Sydney's nightlife offers something for everyone

Oxford Street, with its huge selection of bars and clubs, is a perennial favourite for both gay and straight nightlife. Gilligans in the Oxford Hotel is a fashionable cocktail bar, Midnight Shift, 85 Oxford Street, is a quirky and extravagant nightclub, and the Stonewall Hotel, 175 Oxford Street, offers drag shows and top DJs in an old colonial building. **Kings Cross** is also worth a look. Try The Lincoln, 36 Bayswater Road, or Hugo's Lounge, 33 Bayswater Road. In the **CBD**, popular nightclubs include Gas, 467–477 Pitt Street (near Chinatown); Tank, 3 Bridge Lane (near Martin Place); and Home, at Cockle Bay Wharf, Darling Harbour.

Casino. The Star City casino complex is located in Pyrmont, just around the corner from Darling Harbour and not far from the National Maritime Museum. The casino has some special Aussie touches, such as two vast aquariums designed to impart a Great Barrier Reef feel, and an Outback area, with a replica of Wave Rock (a Western Australian landmark).

The Star City complex also offers other kinds of entertainment too. The Lyric Theatre features top stage productions and the showroom presents various cabaret acts.

The Entertainment Quarter. This complex on Lang Road near Centennial Park (www.eqmoorepark.com.au) contains cinemas, and plenty of cafés, restaurants and bars.

CHILDREN'S SYDNEY

Sydney has many activities on offer that will engage even the most demanding kids. Several child-friendly attractions are conveniently located in **Darling Harbour** *(see pages 48–52)*: the monorail (kids love it), Sydney Aquarium, Sydney Wildlife World, Tumbalong Park and, for older children, the Imax Theatre, the Powerhouse Museum and the Maritime Museum. **Taronga Zoo** *(see page 28)* and **Featherdale Wildlife Park** *(see page 65)* appeal to kids of all ages. The 'Search and Discover' section on the second floor of the **Australian Museum** *(see page 47)* lets children get their hands on all sorts of exciting exhibits. **Luna Park** is a compact theme park at Milsons Point, near the northern end of

Kids love Sydney Aquarium

the Harbour Bridge. The **Opera House** *(see page 36)* runs children's events such as the Babies Proms, which allows toddlers to get close to the musical instruments (tel: 02 9250-7111). The **Art Gallery of New South Wales** *(see page 40)* holds special family events on Sundays, such as renditions of Aboriginal Dreamtime stories (tel: 02 9225-1700).

Calendar of Events

January. Sydney Festival: a month of Australian and international music, dance, theatre and the visual arts. Big Day Out: alternative music festival at Sydney Showground. Manly Surf Carnival: surf carnival attracting thousands of entrants at Manly Beach. Australia Day: 26 January, celebration of Australia's national day, with various events at Darling Harbour and a ferry race on Sydney Harbour.

March–April. Sydney Gay and Lesbian Mardi Gras Parade: fun-filled, provocative parade along Oxford Street. Sydney Cup: major Sydney horse race, held at Randwick Racecourse. Royal Easter Show: agricultural displays and carnival rides at Sydney Olympic Park. Anzac Day parade (25 April): old soldiers march down George Street to remember Australians killed in war. Canberra Balloon Fiesta: more than 60 hot-air balloons take to the skies over the nation's capital in April.

May. Sydney Writers' Festival: major literary festival attracting Australian and international authors.

June. Sydney Biennale: contemporary visual arts festival held in even-numbered years. Sydney Film Festival: major Australian film festival. Sydney Good Food and Wine Fair, held at Darling Harbour.

August. City to Surf fun run: thousands of contestants run from the city to Bondi Beach, a distance of about 14km (8¾ miles).

September. Festival of the Winds: kite-flying festival held at Bondi Beach.

October. Manly International Jazz Festival. Good Food Month: celebrating the food and wine industries of New South Wales at various central city locations. Floriade (Canberra): month-long festival of spring flowers.

November. Sculpture by the Sea: outdoor sculpture exhibition along the walking track from Bondi to Bronte.

December. Homebake: Sydney's major rock festival, held in The Domain. Sydney to Hobart yacht race: one of the world's toughest yacht races starting on Boxing Day. New Year's Eve: spectacular fireworks displays on the harbour, plus raucous celebrations in The Rocks and elsewhere in the city.

EATING OUT

Modern Australian cuisine – sometimes called 'Mod Oz' – takes fresh, high-quality ingredients and combines them with culinary approaches and techniques borrowed from all over the world. The British chef and food writer Rick Stein has remarked on Sydney's dynamic food culture and its two main influences: the various ethnic groups that make up the population and a climate that allows a wide range of food to be cultivated locally.

What to Eat and Drink

Immigrants from a dozen or so countries have helped revolutionise the urban Sydney diet, transforming it, over a period of 40 years, from basic meat-and-veg fodder to what has been described as fusion food (a collage of culinary influences encompassing Asian, Mediterranean and Middle Eastern). Australian chefs have propelled the national taste buds into uncharted waters, experimenting widely and mixing the cuisines of Asia and Europe.

Chefs in Sydney have the advantage of being able to work with superb raw materials. Australia's size and climatic diversity make it possible to produce an astonishing variety of fruits and vegetables – apples, lychees, mandarins, custard apples, mangoes, strawberries, blackberries, passionfruit, pumpkin (squash) and bok choy – to name just a few. Top-quality meat and a wide range of super-fresh seafood add to the classy culinary mix. A lot of these ingredients are seasonal or have to be freighted long distances, of course, so the situation isn't quite perfect, but chefs never have to look too far to find ingredients that combine to produce astounding results that would be hard to duplicate anywhere else in the world.

Sydney seafood

Dining in Sydney can be as expensive as you want it to be. Foodies agree that the city's top-level restaurants compare in quality to the best restaurants of New York, Paris and London – with prices to match. Pretty much any establishment that offers a view of the harbour will be considerably more expensive than a restaurant of similar quality lacking a view. But the good news is, it doesn't have to cost a lot to eat well. Moderately priced restaurants abound in Sydney, especially in the inner suburbs. Note that smoking is banned in all restaurants.

Bush Tucker

Australian chefs often try to incorporate native foods into their dishes. Ingredients such as muntari berries, bush tomatoes, Illawarra plums, lemon myrtle and lilli pillies have begun to appear on restaurant menus, often blended with traditional dishes of meat and fish. This native food of Australia – the fruits, seeds, nuts, fungi, mammals, reptiles, fish and birds that sustained Aborigines for tens of thousands of years – is referred to collectively as 'bush tucker'. Popular ingredients include quandongs (similar to a peach but with a rhubarb-like tang), wattle seeds (sometimes used in ice cream to give a coffee-like flavour), Kakadu plums (less sweet than the usual variety) and bunya bunya nuts (delicious in satay sauces). Kangaroo, crocodile and emu (a relative of the ostrich) have also found their way onto many menus; all three are commercially farmed and are low in fat. Two Aboriginal foods that have yet to become popular in Sydney restaurants – and let's face it, probably never will – are witchetty grubs (large grubs found in the trunks and roots of wattle trees) and bogong moths (a hefty migratory moth, usually roasted in a fire and eaten like peanuts).

First vines

Australia's interest in wine production goes back a couple of centuries. The founder of the New South Wales colony, Governor Arthur Phillip, certainly had his priorities right, and one of the first projects he ordered in 1788 was the planting of grapevines at Sydney Cove.

Australian Wines

Australian wines are among the world's best – a judgement confirmed regularly at international wine shows. The Australian wine industry is aiming to become the world's most profitable and influential supplier of branded wines within 30 years, a target that assumes a massive increase in the value of

Australia's wine exports. Wine is produced in every state in Australia over a great range of climatic and soil conditions. Riesling, Chardonnay and Semillon are the most favoured white varieties, while popular reds include Cabernet Sauvignon, Merlot, Pinot Noir and Shiraz (also known in Europe as Syrah).

Many of Sydney's less expensive restaurants are BYO (bring your own), but bottle shops (off licences) are not hard to find and most offer a wide selection at very moderate prices. A number of the fully licensed restaurants have very well chosen wine cellars *(see page 137)*.

Fine Australian wine and fine Australian service

The Amber Nectar

Beer (aka the amber nectar) is served cold, sometimes very cold. Australia's best-known beer is probably Fosters lager, but there are many more. Reschs, Tooheys and VB (Victoria Bitter) are big-selling brands in Sydney bars. Some beers are sold in 'new' and 'old' varieties, the first being lager, the latter darker in colour. The alcoholic strength of Australian beer must by law be displayed on the can or bottle. Full strength draught beer is around 4.9 percent alcohol, 'mid-strength' beer will be around 3.5 percent alcohol and beers marked 'light' will be no more than 2.7 percent alcohol.

'Boutique' beers, brewed in smaller batches, are popular. Redoak is a good example. Other, more commercial premium brands include Hahn, James Boag and Cascade. Coopers Ale, brewed in South Australia, has a loyal following. Coopers is more like a British beer (but colder) and pretty strong, at 5.8 percent alcohol.

A 285ml (10-ounce) beer glass is called a 'middie' in New South Wales and a 425ml (15-ounce) glass is called a 'schooner'. A small bottle of beer is known throughout Australia as a 'stubbie'. An off licence is called a bottle shop, or 'bottle-o'. To 'shout' someone a drink means to buy them one, as in, 'Can I shout you a drink?' Pub patrons may be 'in a shout', which means they are with a group of drinkers who take turns to buy drinks for the whole group.

Where to Eat

Some of Sydney's most acclaimed restaurants are to be found in The Rocks, around Circular Quay and in the CBD. There are a some good, less expensive options at Darling Harbour and the adjoining Cockle Bay and King Street wharves. Don't limit your dining to these areas, though, because many other neighbourhoods and suburbs such as Kings Cross, Surry Hills,

A Drop for Connoisseurs

Above the Argyle Cut, at 100 Cumberland Street, the Australian Hotel is well worth a visit. A friendly pub in the older Aussie tradition, it stocks beers from every state in the country, including a few eagerly sought by connoisseurs. The Australian is one of only two pubs in Sydney to serve unfiltered beers created by master brewer Geoff Scharer. These include Picton Lager (5 percent alcohol) and the celebrated Bavarian-style Burragorang Bock (6.4 percent), acclaimed by expert tasters and seasoned journalists as possibly the best beer in Australia.

Alfresco dining at Circular Quay

Darlinghurst, Paddington and Newtown offer exciting options as well. Oxford Street in Darlinghurst, for example, is lined with smaller restaurants, many of which offer outstanding cuisine and seafood at moderate prices. The largest concentration is in the block immediately east of Taylor Square; really more of a crossroads than a square, the neighbourhood is a bit scruffy, but there are many good restaurants here.

Crown Street, which heads off Oxford Street a block west of Taylor Square, is a popular eating haunt. You'll soon come to Surry Hills, which boasts Japanese restaurants, Turkish pide (pizza) houses, Indian restaurants, a gourmet wood-fired pizza outlet, Thai restaurants and several fine-dining establishments. Around the corner in Cleveland Street (towards the corner of Elizabeth Street) is a cluster of good-value Lebanese restaurants.

Other areas worth exploring when you're hungry include Kings Cross and Potts Point, which are peppered with stylish

Two of the best

You get world-class cooking at Tetsuya's (see page 139) and Rockpool (see page 138). Both restaurants were among the 50 Best Restaurants in the World for 2008 listed by the respected *Restaurant Magazine*.

restaurants and funky cafés, particularly along Victoria Street; East Sydney near the Central Business District, noted for its Italian and Mod Oz eateries; and the Inner West suburb of Newtown, which has a large concentration of inexpensive restaurants – everything from Greek, Italian and Chinese to Turkish, Mongolian and Thai. Italian cuisine dominates the eating-out scene in Leichhardt and Haberfield, also in the Inner West. Bondi Beach to the east of the CBD is renowned for its profusion of seafood and modern Australian restaurants. On the North Shore, Crows Nest, McMahon's Point and Kirribilli are the best bets.

Sydney Fish Market

Sydney's bustling fish market, on Blackwattle Bay in Pyrmont (just west of Darling Harbour), is well worth a visit. Australian tuna, Tasmanian salmon and blue swimmer crabs are air-freighted from here to Japan, where they appear on the auction block at Tokyo's Tsukiji Market not long after they are hauled from the sea. But much of the daily catch stays right in Sydney, to be sold at the market's daily early-morning auction (wholesale only) or throughout the day at the many retail outlets that line the wharf. You can easily put together a fine seafood meal by grazing your way past the sushi bars, fish cafés and vendors offering everything from fresh, ice-cold raw oysters to grilled mixed-seafood platters (prepared alfresco). One of the best-value lunches is the simplest. Just ask for a kilo (2.2lbs) of large cooked prawns (shrimps) and pick a bottle of crisp white wine from a bottle shop. Grab a seat at one of the tables on the dock and savour your meal while boats bob at anchor and pelicans soar overhead.

There are few places in the world where you'll be able to see as many types of freshwater fish, saltwater fish and shellfish amassed in one place. The displays are overwhelming and many visitors find it hard to choose. Be adventurous and try something new, like 'bugs', for example. Balmain bugs are a type of saltwater crustacean, similar to crayfish; they're highly favoured by Sydneysiders. Other popular choices are yabbies (native freshwater crayfish), Tasmanian lobsters, baby octopus, freshwater barramundi and king prawns (shrimp). You might even come across crocodile fillets from Darwin.

You can easily walk to the fish market from Darling Harbour. A pleasant alternative is to hop on one of the trams of the Light Rail system, which runs from Central Station.

A fresh catch at Sydney Fish Market

HANDY TRAVEL TIPS

An A–Z Summary of Practical Information

A

ACCOMMODATION (see also CAMPING and YOUTH HOSTELS)

Accommodation in Sydney ranges from hostels and rooms above pubs to large international hotels. Large five-star hotels in central Sydney include the Four Seasons, the Shangri-La Sydney, the Sheraton on the Park, the Westin Sydney, the Sebel Pier One, the Sir Stamford at Circular Quay, the Hilton and the Sofitel Wentworth.

Overseas offices of Tourism Australia (www.australia.com) have listings of hotels and motels. You can reserve accommodation through your travel agent or airline. Within Australia, book through the state tourist offices, domestic airlines, hotel chains or through online providers such as Wotif (www.wotif.com). Accommodation may be harder to find during the Australian school holidays. These are staggered state by state except for the year-end period (December–February) when schools everywhere close. Tourism Australia offices can provide details *(see page 127)*.

AIRPORT

Sydney Airport (www.sydneyairport.com.au), about 8km (5 miles) from the city centre, is Australia's busiest international airport. It has been upgraded over the past few years to offer more shops, restaurants, bars and open space. The domestic and international terminals are a shuttle-bus ride apart. There is a railway line between the airport and Sydney's Central Station. This 10-km (6-mile) Airport Link (tel: 131 500; www.airportlink.com.au) has five stations, including one at Sydney Airport's international terminal and another at the domestic terminal. There is also a freeway linking central Sydney with the airport.

Arriving passengers can travel from Sydney Airport to town by taxi (20 minutes), train (10 minutes) or bus (20–30 minutes). The Airporter bus service (tel: 02 9666-9988; www.kst.com.au) goes to the door of major hotels.

B

BICYCLE HIRE

Cars clog Sydney's roads and attempts by the traffic authorities to cater to Sydney's sizeable cycling fraternity have often resulted in little more than cosmetic changes. Bicycle lanes are marked on some inner-city roads, but most drivers ignore them. Many drain covers have slots that run parallel to the kerb, so cycle carefully. You can hire a bike or sign up for a tour that includes transport to and from a scenic area (bikes provided), food and accommodation. Cyclists must by law wear helmets. Contact Bicycle New South Wales for more information (tel: 02 9218-5400, www.bicyclensw.org.au).

BUDGETING FOR YOUR TRIP

The basics – food, accommodation, admission charges – are still comparatively inexpensive. A plate of noodles or pasta in an average restaurant costs about A$15. A bottle of Australian wine from a bottle shop (off licence) starts at about $10, a 260ml glass of beer in a pub costs from A$3 and a cup of coffee or tea costs about A$2.80. Entry to a museum or art gallery ranges from free up to A$15 per person.

Transport costs. Air travel to Australia is still relatively expensive, but domestic airfares have fallen lately, thanks to competition between Qantas, its low-cost offshoot Jetstar, Virgin Blue and Tiger Air. A return flight to Canberra costs A$60–200. International passengers may be entitled to discounted travel within Australia, depending on their airline and type of fare. On the ground, train travel can be competitive over shorter distances. Countrylink (www.countrylink.info), the NSW State Rail service, offers an adult economy return trip to Canberra for about A$100. Coach travel is generally cheaper – try Greyhound Australia (www.greyhound.com.au).

The rough cost of a half-day coach sightseeing tour is A$55–60 per person. A tour of the Blue Mountains costs A$80–150.

The cost of a litre of petrol (gasoline) is approximately A$1.50, more expensive than in the US but cheaper than in most European countries. Hiring a small car costs from A$65 per day and hiring a camper van (sleeping two) costs about A$110 per day. Caravan park sites often charge less than A$25 a night.

Accommodation. A room at a backpacker hostel costs A$35–100 per night. Rooms at five-star hotels start at A$350 per night. Sydney has a range of lodging options in between *(see pages 129–136)*.

C

CAMPING

Australians are avid campers, and you'll find campsites all over the country. The sites tend to be packed during school holidays. They all have at least the basic amenities, and in some cases much more in the way of comfort. Aside from roomy tents with lights and floors, some installations have caravans (trailers) or cabins. Showers, toilets, laundry facilities and barbecue grills are commonly available. Sheets and blankets can often be hired. The national parks generally have well-organised camping facilities. To camp beyond the designated zone you must ask rangers for permission. The Basin scenic campsite on the shore of Pittwater in Ku-ring-gai Chase National Park, quite close to the city, is a favourite. Many coach tours include camping segments, or you can hire a camper van or motor home by the day or week *(see below)*.

CAR HIRE

In inner-city Sydney, with its traffic jams and parking hassles, a car is a burden. To see the surrounding countryside at your own pace, however, there's no substitute for a car or a four-wheel-drive vehicle. Competition among international and local car rental companies means you can often find special deals. Unlimited mileage is common, and there are often weekend discounts.

If you intend to drive in remote country areas, rates may be considerably higher. It's worth shopping around, but be careful – some companies impose a metropolitan limit on vehicles. Check first, as your insurance won't be valid outside the designated area.

To hire a car you'll need a current driving licence. The minimum age is 21, or in some cases 25. Third-party insurance is included; collision damage and personal accident insurance will cost extra.

Big firms such as Avis, Hertz, Thrifty and Budget offer interstate arrangements where you pick up a car in one city and return it elsewhere. Camper vans and caravans are available, though many are reserved far in advance for school holiday periods.

CLIMATE

Sydney enjoys a temperate and pleasant climate. It's not perfect; the downside is late-summer humidity, which runs at an average 69 percent and makes Sydney the most humid Australian city outside tropical Darwin. Ocean breezes help cool Sydney's coastal suburbs.

Seasons are the reverse of those in the northern hemisphere, with winter running from June to August. Rain tends to fall in intense, tropical bursts in summer. February and March are sultry months, ideal for mosquitoes. April and May are more pleasant months. The NSW outback is mostly very hot from December to February. Average Sydney temperatures are as follows:

	J	F	M	A	M	J	J	A	S	O	N	D
Max°C	26	26	25	22	19	17	16	18	20	22	24	25
Min °C	18	19	17	15	11	9	8	9	11	13	15	17
Max°F	79	79	77	72	66	63	61	64	68	72	75	77
Min °F	64	66	63	59	52	48	46	48	52	55	59	63
Ocean temperature												
°C	22	22	22	21	14	17	16	16	16	17	19	20
°F	72	72	72	70	58	63	61	61	61	63	66	68

CLOTHING

Whatever your itinerary, whatever the season, forget an overcoat, though a light raincoat will serve in almost any season. A sweater or fleece will come in handy in winter. Anywhere you go you'll need comfortable walking shoes. While Sydneysiders dress casually at weekends, business attire can be surprisingly conservative.

Restaurants do not require men to wear a jacket and tie, but some may refuse customers wearing T-shirts, vest tops, ripped jeans or thongs (flip-flops). Entering nightclubs generally requires a collared shirt and smart shoes – not trainers or flip-flops.

CRIME AND SAFETY

Sydney's murder rate is low by world standards and the city is generally safe. It's still wise to take precautions against burglary and petty theft. Place your valuables in a hotel's safe deposit box or in-room safe. Lock your room and your car. Be on the alert for pickpockets on crowded buses and in markets.

Muggings and fights sometimes happen. It's better to avoid Hyde Park after dark, particularly if on your own. William Street, which runs from Hyde Park to Kings Cross, is another place where it's unwise to loiter after dark. The secluded back streets of Kings Cross have a similar reputation, although the main strip is safe enough. Police report instances of bag snatching and fights around the Redfern Station and Waterloo areas in inner-southern Sydney.

CUSTOMS AND ENTRY REQUIREMENTS

Australia requires all visitors to hold a visa. Citizens of New Zealand receive an automatic electronic visa when they present their passports at the Immigration counter.

Australia's Electronic Travel Authority (ETA) allows travel agents to issue an 'invisible visa' electronically to visitors at time of booking in their home countries. You can also apply yourself via the internet at www.eta.immi.gov.au; a small fee applies.

The ETA eliminates having to find an embassy or consulate. Tourists or travellers visiting friends or relatives and wishing to stay for up to three months on each visit within a 12-month period should apply for the Visitor/Tourist ETA. Those making a business visit of less than three months should apply for a Short Validity Business ETA.

If you wish to extend your stay beyond three months, you will need to contact the nearest office of the Department of Immigration and Multicultural Affairs before your three-month stay period is up.

Australia operates reciprocal working holiday schemes with Canada, Ireland, Japan, Korea, Malta, the Netherlands, Germany, Denmark, Sweden, Norway, the UK and some other countries, for applicants between 18 and 30, either single or married without children. Working holiday visas allow recipients to work for up to three months at a time, over a one-year period. For more information, see the Department of Immigration website, www.immi.gov.au.

Entry formalities. On the last leg of your flight to Australia you'll be asked to complete a customs form, swearing that you are not trying to import foreign foodstuffs (including fresh fruit), weapons, drugs or other forbidden articles. There is also an Immigration form. Vaccinations are not required unless you have come from or visited a yellow fever-infected country or zone within six days prior to arrival. You may be required to show your return or onward ticket, and you may need to prove that your funds are sufficient to last out your planned stay. Note that the Quarantine Service uses sniffer dogs at the airport baggage reclaim area to detect banned foodstuffs, including fresh fruit.

Exit formalities. You'll need to fill out a departure form for the Immigration authorities. If you are carrying A$10,000 or more in foreign currency, you must declare it to Customs.

Duty-free. Anyone over the age of 18 is allowed to bring into Australia A$900 worth of goods not including alcohol or tobacco; 2.25 litres of alcohol (including wine, beer or spirits) and 250 cigarettes or 250 grams of cigars or tobacco products other than cigarettes.

D

DRIVING

Australians drive on the left and pass on the right. Australian roads are good considering the size of the country and the challenges of distance, terrain and climate. Freeways and motorways link populous regions, but most country roads are single-lane (that is, one lane in each direction), which can be crowded at busy times. Within Sydney, freeways (marked with an 'F') are toll-free; motorways ('M') have a toll.

Regulations. Drivers and passengers must wear seat belts. (The exception is on buses and coaches, although many of them have seat belts.) Car-hire companies can supply suitable child restraints, boosters, and baby capsules and seats, at an extra charge. A tourist may drive in Australia on a valid overseas licence for the same class of vehicle. Licences must be carried when driving. If the licence is in a language other than English, the visitor must carry a translation. An International Drivers Permit is not sufficient by itself.

Speed limits are signposted. In cities, the speed limit is generally 60km/h (about 35mph), but on suburban streets it is usually 50km/h (about 30mph). In the NSW countryside, the limit is 100 or 110km/h (about 70mph). Police make random checks for drugs or alcohol, using breath tests. The limit on alcohol in the blood is 0.05, meaning in practice that two or three glasses of wine or two or three medium-size ('middy') glasses of beer in an hour will take you to the limit. If you are under 25 and in your first three years of driving, you must be under 0.02, which doesn't allow you to drink at all.

City driving. Heavy traffic and parking problems afflict the central city area, which might explain why Sydney drivers are so impatient and why they tend (when road conditions permit) to drive too fast. Parking meters and 'no standing' zones proliferate.

Outback driving. Thoroughly check the condition of your car and be sure you have a spare wheel and plenty of spare drinking water. Find out about the fuel situation in advance and always leave word as to your destination and anticipated arrival time. Fill up the fuel tank at every opportunity, as the next station may be a few hundred kilometres away. Obtain local knowledge about the road conditions. Some dirt roads are so smooth you may be tempted to speed, but conditions can change abruptly. Be cautious with road trains, consisting of three or four huge trailers barrelling down the motorway towed by a high-powered truck. Pass one, if you dare, with the greatest of care.

Fuel. Many filling stations are open only during normal shopping hours, so you may have to ask where out-of-hours service is available. Petrol (gasoline) in Australia comes in unleaded regular and premium unleaded grades, and is sold by the litre. In 2008, a litre of petrol cost about A$1.50. Prices are often higher in country areas. Most stations are self-service and accept international credit cards.

Road signs. Signs are generally good, especially along heavily used roads. All distances are measured in kilometres. White-on-brown direction signs signal tourist attractions and natural wonders. To drive into the centre of any city, follow the signs marked 'City'; leaving is less straightforward: exit routes are often signposted with the assumption that every driver has local experience, so you may need a good map and some advance planning. Most road signs are the standard international pictographs, but some are unique to Australia, such as silhouette images of kangaroos or wombats, warning that you may encounter these animals crossing the road. Some other signs unique to Australia include:

Crest	Hilltop limiting visibility
Cyclist hazard	Dangerous for cyclists
Dip	Severe depression in road surface
Hump	Bump or speed obstacle
Safety Ramp	Uphill escape lane from a steep downhill road
Soft Edges	Soft shoulders

E

ELECTRICITY

The standard throughout Australia is 230–250 volt, 50-cycle AC. Plugs are three-pronged, in the shape of a bird's footprint, like those used in New Zealand. If you're from elsewhere, you'll need an adapter. Many hotel rooms also have 110-volt outlets for razors and small appliances.

EMBASSIES AND CONSULATES

The embassies or high commissions of about 70 countries are established in Canberra, the national capital. They have consular sections dealing with such things as passport renewal, visas and other formalities. More than 40 countries also have diplomatic representation in Sydney.

The following consulates are in Sydney:

Canada: Level 5, Quay West Building, 111 Harrington Street; tel: 02 9364-3000.

Ireland: Level 26, 1 Market Street, tel: 02 9264-9635.

New Zealand: Level 10, 55 Hunter Street; tel: 02 8256-2000.

UK: Level 16, The Gateway, 1 Macquarie Place; tel: 02 9247-7521.

US: Level 59, MLC Centre, 19-29 Martin Place; tel: 02 9373-9200.

EMERGENCIES

For an ambulance, the fire department, or the police, dial **000**. This number is free to dial from public telephones. You can also dial 112 if using a mobile phone.

G

GAY AND LESBIAN TRAVELLERS

Sydney is one of the world's major gay cities, sometimes called 'the Gay Capital of the Southern Hemisphere'. It's certainly the gay and lesbian capital of Australia. Estimates of the gay population vary, but 400,000 is commonly quoted, which would make one Sydneysider in 10 gay. NSW has outlawed vilification of gays, or discrimination against them, although intolerance still exists.

The main gay weekly publication is the *Sydney Star Observer* (www.ssonet.com.au). Obtainable from bookshops, pubs and cafés throughout inner Sydney, it contains news and information on gay events and venues.

Sydney's main gay district is Oxford Street (sometimes called 'the Golden Mile') and the surrounding Darlinghurst area. Another neighbourhood with a fairly strong gay scene is King Street in Newtown. Well-known pubs around Oxford Street favoured by the male gay community include the Beauchamp, the Oxford and the Beresford. In Newtown, men congregate at the Imperial Hotel and the Newtown Hotel, while lesbians hang out at the Bank Hotel.

GETTING THERE

By air. Flights from Asia, North America and Europe serve international airports around Australia, of which Sydney's is the busiest. Australia is included in several 'round-the-world' fare schemes – arrangements between two or more airlines that allow passengers to travel globally at bargain rates, provided they keep to a certain mileage and number of stop-overs. One such fare, Global Explorer, combines the services of Qantas, British Airways and American Airlines, covering 600 destinations worldwide. Flight times (approximate) are New York–Sydney, 22 hours; Los Angeles–Sydney, 15 hours; London–Sydney, 21 hours. You can usually break the flight for a day or two at one of the stops along the way; in most cases this doesn't affect the price of the air ticket.

By sea. Sydney features in the itineraries of many cruise ships. You can fly to, say, Bali or Singapore and embark on the liner there, sail to Australia, then fly home from any Australian city, or resume the cruise at another port.

GUIDES AND TOURS

Tour companies offer a broad choice of excursions, from half a day in Sydney to long-haul journeys into the Outback. Harbour cruises range from the general sightseeing tour to specialised visits to historic Fort Denison. There are also local walking tours – around The Rocks, for instance – and tours for cyclists, wildlife-lovers and others with special interests. Contact the Sydney Visitors Centre *(see page 127)* for information, or see www.visitnsw.com.au.

H

HEALTH AND MEDICAL CARE

Standards of hygiene are high, particularly in food preparation. Doctors and dentists are proficient and hospitals well equipped. If you fall ill, your hotel can call a doctor or refer you to one, or you can ask your embassy, high commission or consulate for a list of approved doctors. You should take out health insurance before departure to cover your stay in Australia. Also ensure you have personal insurance or travel insurance with a comprehensive health component to cover the possibility of illness or accident.

Medicare, Australia's national health insurance scheme, covers visitors from New Zealand, the UK, Ireland and some other European countries. To be eligible, contact your health service before travelling to Australia to ensure you have the correct documents should you need to enrol at a Medicare office (you can enrol before or after you receive treatment). The agreement covers urgent treatment but not elective surgery, dental care, ambulance services, illness arising en-route to Australia or repatriation in the case of serious illness or injury.

You are allowed to bring 'reasonable quantities' of prescribed non-narcotic medications. All should be clearly labelled and identifiable and carried in personal hand luggage. For large quantities, bring a doctor's certificate to produce at Customs if necessary.

Local pharmacies can fill prescriptions written by an Australian-registered doctor.

Health hazards. Ultraviolet levels are high and the onset of sun-burn can be rapid; high-factor protective cream is essential if exposed, even on cloudy days.

Further afield, poisonous snakes and spiders lurk. You are unlike-ly to encounter snakes in central Sydney, but they sometimes crop up in the outer suburbs. Most dangerous are death adders. The Sydney funnelweb spider, dark and bulbous, is one of the world's most lethal. An antivenom has been developed. The spider lives in holes in the ground, chiefly in Sydney's northern suburbs. Bites are rare (about 10 victims a year) and require immediate medical attention. Catch the spider for identification if you can. Other poisonous spiders include the redback, the eastern mouse spider, and the white-tail. Bites from these are rare and seldom lethal, but see a doctor if bitten.

Shark attacks are extremely rare. In certain seasons and areas, bluebottles (also called Portuguese man o' war) may cluster. The sting is painful but can be treated with hot (not boiling) water.

Sydney has Australia's highest rate of AIDS-related deaths, so protect yourself from exposure to sexually transmitted diseases.

HOLIDAYS

1 January	*New Year's Day*
26 January	*Australia Day*
March/April	*Good Friday, Holy Saturday, Easter Monday*
25 April	*Anzac Day*
June (2nd Monday)	*Queen's Birthday*
October (1st Monday)	*Labour Day*
25 December	*Christmas Day*
26 December	*Boxing Day*

School holidays arrive four times a year, the longest one being in the summer through the latter part of December and all January.

LANGUAGE

Australian is spoken everywhere. The vernacular is sometimes called *Strine,* which is how the word 'Australian' sounds in an extreme Australian pronunciation. Educated and cultivated Australians tend to speak in more neutral tones; a strong Australian accent can sound to an American or European ear like a profound Cockney accent piped through the nose. Foreigners who listen carefully usually understand what's said, at least when it's repeated.

LAUNDRY AND DRY CLEANING

Hotels and motels usually offer same-day laundry and dry-cleaning services for guests, though they tend to be quite expensive. Many hotels and motels also have do-it-yourself washers and dryers on the premises, as well as irons and ironing boards in the rooms.

MAPS

State and local tourist offices give away useful maps of their areas, and there are free specialised maps, of Darling Harbour, for instance, or the Sydney ferry network. Car-hire companies often supply free city directories showing each street and place of interest. For more detailed maps, it may be worth buying a *Gregory's Street Directory.*

MEDIA

Newspapers. Sydney's biggest-selling daily, the *Sydney Morning Herald*, publishes a TV guide on Mondays, a restaurant and cooking guide called Good Living on Tuesdays, and an entertainment guide called Metro on Fridays. Other daily papers are the *Daily Telegraph,* the *Australian,* and the *Australian Financial Review.*

The latter two circulate nationally. Specialist newsstands in Sydney sell newspapers from New York, London, Rome, Paris, Hong Kong and Singapore.

Television. Excluding pay TV, five channels are available: ABC (channel 2) is taxpayer-funded and commercial-free. The commercial channels are channels 7, 9, 10 and SBS. The latter broadcasts foreign films with subtitles, documentaries, European sports and news programmes concentrating on overseas coverage.

Radio. AM stations include ABC Radio National (576AM), which is intelligent and articulate. ABC NewsRadio (630AM) concentrates on worldwide news. 702 ABC Sydney (702AM) is most popular of the ABC (taxpayer funded) stations – good morning news and current affairs. 2UE (945AM) has much talkback. 2KY (1017AM) has a lot of horse racing. Others are 2GB (873AM) and 2CH (1170AM). SBS Radio (1386AM) broadcasts a variety of non-English-language programmes. On the FM band are two classical music stations, 2MBS (102.5FM) and Classic FM (92.9FM). Four popular music FM stations are Triple J (105.7FM), Triple M (104.9FM), WSFM (101.7FM) and Nova (96.9FM).

MONEY

Currency. You don't have to reach for a credit card to pay with plastic in Australia – banknotes (bills) are made of it and feature transparent panels instead of watermarks. The currency is decimal-based, with the dollar as the basic unit (100 cents equals one dollar). Notes come in $100, $50, $20, $10 and $5 denominations. Coins come in 5c, 10c, 20c, 50c, $1 and $2 denominations. Because there are no 1- or 2-cent pieces, when giving change prices are rounded to the nearest 5 cents. As for credit cards, American Express, MasterCard, Visa and Diners Club are widely accepted, but you may encounter problems with them in smaller towns, country areas and small retail shops. Some businesses impose a small credit-card surcharge.

Currency exchange. All international airports in Australia provide currency exchange facilities, and foreign notes or travellers' cheques can be converted at most banks. Cash travellers' cheques at banks or larger hotels, as it may be difficult elsewhere. Some banks may charge a fee for cashing them – Australian banks charge for just about everything these days.

ATMs. Debit cards are widely used and cash machines are widespread. You may be able to obtain cash directly in this way using the same PIN you use at home, provided your card has been validated for international access. Electronic point-of-sale transactions (EFTPOS) are available at larger stores.

OPENING HOURS

Banks. Generally open 9.30am to 4pm Monday to Thursday and 9.30am to 5pm on Fridays. Selected banking facilities my be available on Saturday morning, but don't rely on it. Currency exchange facilities at Sydney Airport are open all hours.

Post offices. Generally open 9am–5pm Monday to Friday; some are open Saturday morning.

Shops. The big department stores are open 9am to 5.30pm Monday to Friday and 9am to 6pm on Saturday and 10am or 11am to 5pm on Sunday. Thursday is late shopping night when stores stay open until 8 or 9pm. Stores in some suburbs are open late on other nights. Shopping centres such as the Queen Victoria Building and Harbourside are open seven days a week.

Bars/pubs/hotels. Licensing hours vary, but a typical schedule would be 10am to 10pm or 11pm Monday to Saturday, with most pubs open by noon on Sunday as well. (Some pubs, such as the Crown on the corner of Cleveland and Crown streets, Surry Hills, never close.) Nightclubs can stay open until the following morning, if the clientele can make it.

P

POLICE

NSW operates its own police force, covering both urban and rural areas. The Australian Federal Police, based in Canberra, has jurisdiction over government property, including airports, and deals with interstate problems like drugs and organised crime. Sydney police are generally helpful and friendly. The emergency number is 000.

POST OFFICES

Post offices are signposted 'Australia Post'. Most open 9am–5pm Mon–Fri, though some suburban offices open on Saturday morning, and the General Post Office (GPO) in Pitt Street near Martin Place is open 8.30am–5.30pm Mon–Fri and 10am–2pm Saturday. This is the main post office for post restante – take ID to pick it up.

Postcards to the US or Europe cost A$1.30 and letters A$2. Local letters cost 50 cents. Stamps are often available at front desks of hotels and motels and at some retail outlets. Postboxes are red with an Australia Post logo. Most post offices have fax facilities, as do hotels.

PUBLIC TRANSPORT

The number to call for information on Sydney's public ferries, buses and trains is **131-500**; www.131500.com.au.

Buses. Buses are a practical option during business hours, but service tapers off after dark. The two main starting points for buses are at Wynyard Park on York Street (for the northern suburbs) and at Circular Quay (all other directions). The fare depends on the distance travelled; single tickets may be purchased from the driver or you can buy a Travelten pass from a newsagent, entitling you to 10 rides. Bus route numbers starting with an 'L' are express services with limited stops. Fares depend on the distance travelled; A$1.80 is the cheapest.

Two bus services, red Sydney Explorer and blue Bondi Explorer, offer great sightseeing value. The first covers all the main central Sydney sights and the second visits the bays, beaches and attractions of the eastern side of town, including Kings Cross and Watsons Bay. Pay the driver A$39 for a day ticket and you can hop on and off as you please. They run frequently. Sydney Passes are good value, offering unlimited rides on both the red and blue sightseeing buses, plus access to the Airport Link trains, rail, state-run buses and all ferry services; the passes are available in three-day (A$110), five-day (A$145) and seven-day (A$165) versions. Alternatively, a Daytripper ticket entitles you to one day's use of most trains, buses and ferries (A$16).

Railway. Sydney's underground railway system (subway) operates from 4.30am to midnight; it's the central unit of a railway network that stretches out to the suburbs. After midnight, the Nightride bus service takes over and runs through the night. Sydney's trains are double-deck, and station platforms are marked with special 'Night safe' areas, to show you which carriages are open (those next to the guard's compartment). Other carriages may be closed after dark. Fares are low by world standards – a single ticket from Circular Quay to Bondi Junction costs A$3.

Monorail. This links the central city and Darling Harbour, and runs every 3–5 minutes. Its operating hours are Mon–Thur 7am–10pm, Fri–Sat 7am–midnight and Sun 8am–10pm. Any part of the route up to one complete loop costs A$4.80.

Light rail. Trams once ran throughout the city to as far away as Bondi Beach. Foolishly, however, Sydney scrapped its trams in the early 1960s. A new-style tram service, renamed 'light rail', is now operating on one route. It costs considerably more per stop that the public railway, but is quite scenic, running every 10–15 minutes from Central Station through Chinatown past Darling Harbour to the Fish Market and a little beyond. Single tickets cost A$3.20–4.20 depending on the length of your journey (tel: 02 8584-5288).

Ferries. A vital part of life in Sydney, with so many commuters continually criss-crossing the harbour, ferries sail between 6am and 11pm daily. Most depart from Circular Quay, providing inexpensive outings for sightseers to Kirribilli, Neutral Bay or Taronga Zoo. A trip to the zoo costs A\$5.20 each way. Ferries or fast JetCats shuttle between Circular Quay and Manly. And the slow but scenic way from Circular Quay to Darling Harbour is by ferry. Water taxis let you set your own itinerary, but they are expensive (tel: 02 9555-8888 or 1300-138-840).

Taxis. You can hail a cab on the street if the orange light on top is lit. Otherwise, go to one of the taxi ranks at shopping centres, transport terminals or big hotels, and take the first taxi in the rank. Or phone for a taxi; tel: 133-300 or 131-008. Meters indicate the fare plus any extras, such as waiting time. Higher tariffs apply 10pm–6am. Australians usually sit next to the taxi driver, but if you prefer the back seat, no offence is taken. It is not customary to tip taxi drivers.

R

RELIGION

The major religion in Australia is Christianity. Of the non-Christian faiths, Buddhists are the largest group, followed by Muslims, Hindus and Jews. To find the church of your choice, check at your hotel desk or look in the Yellow Pages.

T

TAX REFUNDS

A Goods and Services Tax (GST) of 10 percent applies to most purchases. The Tourist Refund Scheme (TRS) allows overseas visitors to claim a limited GST refund as they clear Customs. To qualify for the TRS you need to have spent at least A\$300 (including GST), either at the same store (at the one time or over several occasions – but a single tax invoice for all the goods must be provided), or at several stores, no more than 30 days before you leave Australia. You must also take the goods with you as carry-on luggage.

TELEPHONE

Australia's country code is 61, and the code for Sydney is 2. To call a Sydney number from another country dial your country's international access code, then 612, then the eight-digit number. Australia's telephone network, run by Telstra is sophisticated; you can dial anywhere in the country from almost any phone, even in the Outback, and expect a clear line. Many hotel rooms have phones from which you can dial cross-country (STD) or internationally (IDD). Remember, though, that hotels often add hefty surcharges to the bill.

The minimum cost of a local public pay phone call is 50 cents. Long-distance calls within Australia and International Direct Dialling calls can be made on Telstra public pay phones. Check with the operator for these charges as they vary for distances and the time of day. Public pay phones accept most coins as well as phonecards – pre-paid cards used to make local, STD and IDD calls on public phones. (Some public phones accept only phonecards.) Phonecards are widely sold at newsagents and other shops, and come in denominations of $5, $10 and $20. The Telstra PhoneAway pre-paid card enables you to use virtually any phone in Australia – home and office phones, mobile (cell) phones, hotel and pay phones – all call costs are charged against the card. Credit phones, found at airports, many hotels and several city-centre locations, accept most major credit cards such as AMEX, MasterCard and Visa. To make a reverse-charge (call collect) phone call, phone the International Operator, tel: 1234 or 12455.

Phone books give full dialling instructions and details on emergency services. To reach an overseas number, dial 0011, then the country code of the destination, the area code and the local number.

TICKETS

Tickets bought directly from the box office in advance are generally the cheapest. Alternatively, try one of the major booking agencies, Ticketek, tel: 132-849, www.ticketek.com.au, or Ticketmaster, www.ticketmaster.com.au.

TIME ZONES

Australia has three time zones: New South Wales and Australian Capital Territory operate on Eastern Standard Time (EST). Daylight saving (where the clocks go forward an hour) runs in New South Wales and Australian Capital Territory from the end of October to the first Sunday in April. The chart below shows the time differences between Sydney and various other cities in January and July:

	Los Angeles	New York	London	Sydney	Auckland
Jan	3pm	6pm	11pm	10am	noon
	Fri	Fri	Fri	Sat	Sat
July	5pm	8pm	1am	10am	noon
	Fri	Fri	Sat	Sat	Sat

TIPPING

Tipping is a relatively recent custom and is entirely discretionary. Nobody's livelihood depends on tips. It is not customary to tip taxi drivers, porters at airports or hairdressers. Porters have set charges at railway terminals, but not at hotels. Hotels and restaurants do not usually add service charges to accounts, although some restaurants and cafés add a 10 percent surcharge for service on public holidays. In better-class restaurants, patrons sometimes tip food and drink waiters up to 10 percent of the bill, but only if service is good (if you are ecstatic about the service, make it 15 percent). Tipping is an optional gratuity for good service. It has not developed into a means of subsidising wages. If service is poor or a waiter is surly, don't tip.

TOILETS

Australians manage without euphemisms for 'toilet', though in a country so rich in slang you'll come across some wry synonyms. 'Dunny' is the Outback slang term, but 'washroom', 'restrooms', 'ladies' or 'gents' are all understood. In Sydney, public toilets are often locked after certain hours, but you can generally use the facilities in any pub, cinema or department store without making a purchase. Toilets are usually clean, even in the Outback. Sydney's most ornate toilets are on the ground floor of the State Theatre on Market Street.

TOURIST INFORMATION

To obtain tourist information before you leave home, see the comprehensive Tourism Australia website (www.australia.com); contact them at their head office: Level 18, Darling Park, Tower 2, 201 Sussex Street, Sydney NSW 2000, Australia; tel: 02 9360-1111; fax: 02 9331-6469; or at one of the following overseas offices:

Canada: 111 Peter Street, Suite 630, Toronto, Ontario M5V 2H1; tel: (416) 408-0549; fax: (416) 408-1013.
New Zealand: Level 3, 125 The Strand, Parnell, Auckland 1; tel: (09) 915-2826; fax: (09) 307-3117.
UK: Australia Centre, Australia House, 6th Floor, Melbourne Place/Strand, London WC2B 4LG; tel: (020) 7438-4601; fax: (020) 7240-6690.
US: 6100 Center Drive, Suite 1150, Los Angeles CA 90045; tel: (310) 695-3200; fax: (310) 695-3201.

Once in Sydney, visit the Sydney Visitor Centre (www.sydney visitorcentre.com>), in two locations:
The Rocks: Corner of Argyle & Playfair streets, open daily 9.30am–5.30pm, tel: 02 9240-8788 or 1800-067-676.
Darling Harbour: 33 Wheat Road (behind the Imax Theatre), open daily 9.30am–5.30pm, tel: 1800-067-676.

W

WEBSITES AND INTERNET CAFÉS

Australian Tourist Commission: **www.australia.com**
Darling Harbour: **www.darlingharbour.com**
National Parks in NSW: **www.nationalparks.nsw.gov.au**
Public transport information: **www.131500.com.au**
Sydney City Council: **www.cityofsydney.com.au**
Sydney information finder: **www.sydney.citysearch.com.au**
Sydney Morning Herald: **www.smh.com.au**
Sydney Visitor Centre: **www.sydneyvisitorcentre.com**
The Rocks: **www.therocks.com**
Tourism New South Wales: **www.visitnsw.com.au**

Thera are internet cafés in Kings Cross, Glebe and Newtown, one upstairs at the Hotel Sweeney in the CBD (corner of Clarence and Druitt streets), and others at 545 George Street and 391 Pitt Street.

Y

YOUTH HOSTELS

There are two types of hostel accommodation: privately owned backpacker hostels and YHA Hostels (Youth Hostels Association). Both provide self-catering accommodation from about A$30 a night. The Australian YHA is the largest budget accommodation network, with more than 130 hostels in Australia. 'Youth' is a misnomer, as the hostels are open to all ages and offer sleeping areas, self-catering kitchens, and common rooms where you'll meet fellow travellers. You can join the YHA in your own country or in Australia. Check the YHA website for more details – www.yha.com.au.

Sydney's Y Hotel (www.yhotel.com.au) is technically a YWCA, but you do not need to be young, a woman, or Christian to stay. It's safe, comfortable, pleasant, very centrally located and a very good deal. Normal YMCA/YWCA rules apply.

Recommended Hotels

Sydney has a wide range of accommodation, offering everything from elegant, luxury, five-star hotels with impeccable service to self-contained apartment hotels to back-to-basics, inexpensive hostels. Note that rates tend to fall sharply once you move inland from the popular harbourside neighbourhoods.

The symbols below are a guide to the price of a standard double room with bath or shower, excluding tips; breakfast is not included unless otherwise stated. Prices are based on double occupancy on a midweek night. Many hotels in Sydney offer weekend discounts (of up to 30 percent); be sure to ask when making reservations. All hotels take major credit cards unless otherwise stated. For more information about accommodation in Sydney, see page 107.

$$$$	over A$300
$$$	A$200–300
$$	A$120–200
$	below A$120

THE ROCKS AND CIRCULAR QUAY

Australian Hotel $$ *100 Cumberland Street, The Rocks NSW 2000, tel: 02 9247-2229, fax: 02 9241-3262, www.australianheritage hotel.com.* A lovely old pub built in 1913 with very comfortable rooms offering an inexpensive accommodation option in The Rocks. Bathrooms are shared. The roof terrace has views of the Harbour Bridge and Opera House. Price includes breakfast. 18 rooms.

Bed and Breakfast Sydney Harbour $$–$$$ *140–142 Cumberland Street, The Rocks NSW 2000, tel: 02 9247-1130, fax: 02 9247-1148.* This restored early 20th-century building is located around the corner from the busiest part of The Rocks, and within a 10-minute walk of Circular Quay. The rooms, some of which have harbour views, are nicely fitted out with period furniture, and most have their own bathroom. The cooked breakfasts (included in the price) have been highly praised. 9 rooms.

Four Seasons $$$$ *199 George Street, NSW 2000, tel: 02 9238-0000, fax: 02 9251-2851, www.fourseasons.com/sydney.* One of Sydney's original five-star hotels, the Four Seasons (formerly the Regent) has established a superlative reputation. Personal service is great, the hotel overlooks the harbour and The Rocks district. Kable's, the main restaurant, has an excellent reputation. Wheelchair access. 620 rooms.

Holiday Inn Old Sydney $$$ *55 George Street, NSW 2000, tel: 02 9252-0524, fax: 02 9251-2093, www.ichotelsgroup.com.* Great location in The Rocks, with rooftop heated swimming pool, sauna, spa and secure undercover parking. Wheelchair access. 174 guest rooms.

Hotel Inter-Continental Sydney $$$$ *117 Macquarie Street, NSW 2000, tel: 02 9253-9000, fax: 02 9240-1240, www.ichotelsgroup. com.* In an elegant building that incorporates Sydney's historic Treasury Building, the Inter-Continental combines 19th-century grace with 21st-century comfort. Located on one of the city's stateliest thoroughfares, and within walking distance of the harbour, the Opera House and the Royal Botanic Gardens. Swimming pool, health club, sauna and non-smoking floors. Pierpont's Bar stocks Australia's finest collection of Havana cigars. Wheelchair access. 498 rooms.

Observatory Hotel $$$$ *89–113 Kent Street, Millers Point, NSW 2000, tel: 02 9256-2222, fax: 02 9256-2233, www.observatory hotel.com.au.* Smallish by the standards of five-star establishments but grand and elegant, with a serene grace that suggests the hotel has been welcoming guests for decades. In fact, it was built in the 1990s. There is a huge heated indoor pool and many other sumptuous amenities. On a quiet street within easy walking distance of The Rocks. Wheelchair access. 77 rooms.

Park Hyatt Sydney $$$$ *7 Hickson Road, The Rocks, NSW 2000, tel: 02 9241-1234, fax: 02 9256-1555, www.sydney.park. hyatt.com.* When it comes to location and facilities, this low-rise property is hard to beat. Press a button and the curtains slide open, revealing a view of the Opera House and sailing ships. A rooftop jacuzzi helps you slip into that holiday feeling. Popular with visiting celebrities. Wheelchair access. 158 rooms.

Quay Grand $$$$ *61–69 Macquarie Street, NSW 2000, tel: 02 9256-4000, fax: 02 9256-4040, www.mirvachotels.com.* This all-suite 'contemporary Art-Deco' hotel offers uninterrupted views of Sydney Harbour, the Rocks, the Harbour Bridge, the city and the Royal Botanic Gardens. You can watch Sydney's ferries from the main bar. Wheelchair access. 70 rooms.

Shangri-La Hotel Sydney $$$$ *176 Cumberland Street, The Rocks, NSW 2000, tel: 02 9250-6000, fax: 02 9250-6250, www. shangri-la.com.* All rooms have harbour views and luxurious marble bathrooms. The rooms are spacious and the service is excellent. The bar has celebrated city views. Wheelchair access. 563 rooms.

Sir Stamford at Circular Quay $$$–$$$$ *93 Macquarie Street, NSW 2000, tel: 02 9252-4600, fax: 02 9252-4286, www.stamford. com.au.* Opposite the Royal Botanic Gardens and filled with oil paintings, Persian rugs and similar clubby trappings. Wheelchair access. 105 rooms.

CITY CENTRE

All Seasons Menzies Hotel $$$$ *14 Carrington Street, NSW 2000, tel: 02 9299-1000, fax: 02 9290-3819, www.sydneymenzieshotel. com.au.* One of Sydney's older hotels, the clubby Menzies has a traditional feel, but its spacious rooms, recently renovated, are fitted with all the latest amenities. In the heart of Sydney's downtown area. Wheelchair access. 446 rooms.

Mercure Hotel Sydney on Broadway $$$–$$$$ *818–820 George Street, NSW 2000, tel: 02 9217-6666, fax: 02 9217-6888, http:// mercuresydney.com.au.* On Railway Square, within walking distance of Chinatown and Sydney's major entertainment venues. Sydney Football Stadium and Cricket Ground are also just minutes from the hotel. Contemporary decor throughout. Wheelchair access. 517 rooms.

Oaks Hyde Park Plaza $$$ *38 College Street, NSW 2000, tel: 02 9331-6933, fax: 02 9331-6022, www.theoaksgroup.com.au.* Overlooking the park, this hotel offers a variety of self-contained apartments, ranging from studios to two-bedroom family suites and three-bedroom executive suites. Rates include a light breakfast in bed. The Two Fat Ducks Bar is a pleasant lounge for coffee and drinks. Wheelchair access. 182 rooms.

Sheraton on the Park $$$$ *161 Elizabeth Street, NSW 2000, tel: 02 9286-6000, fax: 02 9286-6686, www.starwoodhotels.com/sheraton.* No harbour views, but you can gaze out on the verdant foliage of Hyde Park. The grand lobby and sweeping staircases are complimented by a modern health club and gym. Slick contemporary decor. Conveniently near Sydney's prime shopping venues and department stores. Wheelchair access. 559 rooms.

Sofitel Wentworth $$$$ *61–101 Phillip Street, NSW 2000, tel: 02 9230-0700, fax: 02 9227-9133, www.sofitel.com.* The Wentworth has long been regarded as one of Sydney's grander establishments. Located in the heart of the CBD, the Wentworth is close to the Opera House, Circular Quay, The Rocks and the Royal Botanic Gardens. 436 rooms.

Sydney Central YHA $ *Pitt Street and Rawson Place, NSW 2000, tel: 02 9218-9000, fax: 02 9218-9099, www.yha.com.au.* Technically a youth hostel, it's also an excellent, centrally located hotel in a heritage building opposite Central Station. A double room with private facilities costs from A$100 per room. Dorm accommodation is also available. The YHA also has a pool, sauna, laundry and self-catering kitchens. Wheelchair access. 144 rooms.

Sydney Hilton $$$$ *488 George Street, NSW 2000, tel: 02 9265-6065, www.hiltonsydney.com.au.* This Hilton International-affiliated property has undergone extensive refurbishment and offers a luxurious level of amenities. The stylish lobby is far classier than the building's exterior would suggest. The ornate Marble Bar downstairs, built in 1893, is a Sydney institution. Wheelchair access. 577 rooms.

Sydney Marriott Hotel $$$–$$$$ *36 College Street, NSW 2010, tel: 02 9361-8400, fax: 02 9361-8599, www.marriot.com*. This hotel overlooks Hyde Park, not far from the Australian Museum. Rooms have abundant amenities – three telephones, remote control TV, individual climate control, iron and ironing board, microwave oven, tea and coffee makers, bathrobes and hairdryer. Spa baths are available. Wheelchair access. 227 rooms.

Vibe Hotel $$ *111 Goulburn Street, NSW 2000, tel: 02 8272 3300, fax: 02 9211 3381, www.vibehotels.com.au*. A good-value hotel located on the eastern side of the CBD near Chinatown and Surry Hills. The modern rooms are bright and cheerful. Pool and gym. Check the website for special offers. 190 rooms.

DARLING HARBOUR

Four Points by Sheraton $$$–$$$$ *161 Sussex Street, NSW 2000, tel: 02 9290-4000, fax: 02 9299-3340, www.starwoodhotels.com/fourpoints*. Australia's largest hotel – its elegant, curved shape facing Darling Harbour belies its size. The Four Points is a short walk or monorail ride from the CBD and Sydney entertainment venues. Its Dundee Arms Pub is a pleasant watering hole. 630 rooms.

Grand Mercure Apartments $$$$ *50 Murray Street, Pyrmont, NSW 2009, tel: 02 9563-6666, www.grandmercuredarlingharbour.com.au*. Stylish two- and three-bedroom serviced apartments with private balconies, full kitchen and laundry. Recreation facilities include an indoor rooftop 25-m (80-ft) lap pool, a spa, gym and sauna. The hotel is in walking distance of Sydney Star Casino, Darling Harbour and Cockle Bay Wharf. Wheelchair access. 121 rooms.

Hotel Ibis Darling Harbour $$–$$$ *70 Murray Street, Pyrmont NSW 2009, tel: 02 9563-0888, fax: 02 9563-0899, www.hotelibis darlingharbour.com.au*. A quick walk from the attractions of Darling Harbour and Cockle Bay Wharf, and the Sydney Light Rail and Monorail trains stop at the hotel door. Easy access to Star City Casino, city-centre shopping and entertainment, Chinatown and Central Station. Wheelchair access. 256 rooms.

Novotel Sydney on Darling Harbour $$$$ *100 Murray Street, Pyrmont, NSW 2009, tel: 02 9934-0000, fax: 02 9934-0099, www.novoteldarlingharbour.com.au.* Overlooks the city skyline from Darling Harbour. Guest facilities include full-size tennis court, outdoor pool, gym and sauna. Wheelchair access. 527 rooms.

Vulcan Hotel $–$$ *500 Wattle Street, Ultimo, NSW 2007, tel: 02 9211-3283, fax: 02 9212-7439, www.vulcanhotelsydney.com.* This converted corner pub, a few minutes' walk from Darling Harbour, has stylishly furnished rooms, all with bathrooms. 30 rooms.

EASTERN SUBURBS

Citigate Sebel Sydney $$–$$$ *28 Albion Street, Surry Hills, tel: 02 9289-0000, fax: 02 9289-0001, www.citigatesebel.com.au.* Close to Central Station, the Citigate offers spacious accommodation a stroll from Oxford Street and Chinatown. Wheelchair access. 270 rooms.

City Crown Motel $–$$ *289 Crown Street, Surry Hills, NSW 2010, tel: 02 9331-2433, fax: 02 9360-7760, www.citycrownmotel.com.au.* A trim, pleasant, family-run property in a trendy street in inner-city Surry Hills, a short stroll from Oxford Street and with plenty of cafés and restaurants around. All rooms have their own bathroom and balcony. 30 rooms.

De Vere Hotel $$–$$$ *44–46 Macleay Street, Potts Point NSW 2011, tel: 02 9358-1211, fax: 02 9358-4685, www.devere.com.au.* A good, comfortable budget choice in the heart of the Potts Point/ Kings Cross entertainment district, and close to city attractions. Some rooms on upper floors have harbour views. 100 rooms.

Hotel 59 $–$$ *59 Bayswater Road, Kings Cross NSW 2011, tel: 02 9360-5900, www.hotel59.com.au.* Located in a quiet section of Bayswater Road, this small hotel offers cheerful, fairly basic rooms that are kept spotlessly clean. Excellent cooked breakfasts. 8 rooms.

The Kirketon $$$$ *229 Darlinghurst Road, Darlinghurst NSW 2010, tel: 02 9332-2011, fax: 02 9332-2499, www.kirketon.com.au.*

Glamorous and funky boutique hotel in the thick of the café, restaurant and clubbing scene of Darlinghurst and Kings Cross. Rooms are sleekly designed and comfortable. Very helpful staff. Owned by the same company that runs the Medusa *(see below)*. 40 rooms.

Medusa $$$–$$$$ *267 Darlinghurst Road, Darlinghurst, NSW 2010, tel: 02 9331-1000, fax: 02 9380-6901, www.medusa.com.au.* A fine example of one of Sydney's boutique hotels, Medusa offers 18 individually designed studios complete with stereo equipment, TV and mini-kitchen. Bold light colours and huge beds. Attentive staff. The reflection pool in the courtyard is delightful. 18 rooms.

Oxford Koala Hotel and Apartments $$ *55 Oxford Street, Darlinghurst, NSW 2010, tel: 02 9269-0645, fax: 02 9283-2741.* Close to Hyde Park and the city centre, this large hotel is on the route of Sydney's famous Gay and Lesbian Mardi Gras parade. Rooftop pool, parking and a restaurant. Wheelchair access. 330 rooms.

Regent's Court Hotel $$$–$$$$ *18 Springfield Avenue, Potts Point, NSW 2011, tel: 02 9358-1533, fax: 02 9358-1833, www.regents court.com.* A gorgeous boutique hotel featuring suites with well-stocked kitchens. The building dates back to the 1920s, and the hotel kept to the spirit of that era in a stylish renovation. 29 rooms.

Stamford Plaza Double Bay $$$ *33 Cross Street, Double Bay, NSW 2028, tel: 02 9362-4455, fax: 02 9362-4744, www.stamford. com.au.* Situated in leafy and pleasant Double Bay, a posh residential suburb, this inviting luxury property is just two blocks from the harbour. Stunning views from the rooftop pool, and plenty of restaurants nearby. They do good last-minute deals. Wheelchair access. 106 rooms.

Victoria Court Sydney $–$$ *122 Victoria Street, Potts Point NSW 2011, tel: 02 9357-3200, fax: 02 9357-7606, www.victoriacourt. com.au.* Two neighbouring Victorian terraces have been joined and renovated to create this elegant bed and breakfast establishment. Rooms are comfortable and quiet and are decorated with period furniture. Nearby are good cafés and restaurants. 22 rooms.

BONDI

Ravesi's $$$–$$$$ *Corner of Campbell Parade & Hall Street, Bondi Beach NSW 2026, tel: 02 9365-4422, fax: 02 9365-1481, www. ravesis.com.au.* Walk across to the beach for a morning swim from this lovely Bondi beachfront boutique hotel. Rooms are stylishly decorated and vary from compact rooms with no view, to suites with a terrace overlooking the ocean. The hotel's restaurant is highly regarded. 16 rooms.

Swiss-Grand Hotel Bondi Beach $$$$ *Campbell Parade (corner of Beach Road), Bondi Beach, NSW 2026, tel: 02 9365-5666, fax: 02 9130-3545, www.swissgrand.com.au.* Located right next to Bondi Beach, yet central Sydney and the airport are only 15–20 minutes away. Daily live entertainment in the lobby bar. Wheelchair access. Each room is a suite. 203 rooms.

MANLY

Periwinkle Guesthouse on Manly Cove $–$$ *8–19 East Esplanade corner Ashburner Street, Manly NSW 2095, tel: 02 9977-6308, www.periwinkle.citysearch.com.au.* Located on the harbour side of Manly, Periwinkle offers budget accommodation in a restored Victorian-era house close to the Manly ferry, harbour and shops. Rooms are plain but clean and bright, and there is a communal kitchen, a laundry, and pleasant courtyard. Most rooms have a bathroom. 18 rooms.

Sebel Manly Beach Hotel $$$–$$$$ *8–13 South Steyne, Manly Beach NSW 2095, tel: 02 9977-8866, fax: 02 9977-8209, www. mirvachotels.com/sebel.* Manly is a 20-minute ride by JetCat ferry from Circular Quay, but feels much further away. Recently renovated, this comfortable hotel overlooks the southern end of Manly ocean beach, and is a few minutes' walk from the restaurants of the Corso. Rooms with an ocean view are more expensive than the others. Wheelchair access. 83 rooms.

Recommended Restaurants

Sydney restaurants flit into fashion, often to vanish within a few months of opening day. Sometimes the chef departs in a huff, at other times the restaurant's demise remains a mystery. Despite this tendency, numerous restaurants have stood the test of time and established deservedly fine reputations.

The restaurants listed below are arranged alphabetically by location. Prices quoted are per person for a three-course meal excluding drinks and tip. Some restaurants add a small surcharge on Sundays and public holidays. It is always advisable to phone ahead for a reservation, especially in high season. All restarants take major credit cards unless otherwise stated.

$$$	over A$80
$$	A$40–80
$	below A$40

THE ROCKS AND CIRCULAR QUAY

Guillaume at Bennelong $$$ *136 Sydney Opera House, Bennelong Point, tel: 02 9241-1999.* One of the city's best restaurants. Imaginative modern Australian menu in an acclaimed setting. The prime harbourside location, inside the Opera House's third 'shell', is hard to beat.

Heritage Belgian Beer Café $$ *135 Harrington Street, The Rocks, tel: 02 9241-1775.* Belgian beer and hearty food at this popular brasserie-style eatery. Choose from Belgian favourites like mussels and frites or Flemish beef stew. The beer has its own menu, running to some 30 selections.

MCA Café $$ *140 George Street, The Rocks, tel: 02 9241-4253.* Located on the harbour-facing side of the Museum of Contemporary Art, this café-restaurant features contemporary Australian cuisine, especially seafood. Try to get a table on the balcony – the views are sensational. Breakfast and lunch only.

Rockpool (fish) $$$ *107 George Street, The Rocks, tel: 02 9252-1888.* For nearly 20 years one of Sydney's most fashionable eateries, Rockpool serves innovative and excellent seafood cuisine in a stylish setting. Try the stir-fried crab omelette.

Sailor's Thai Canteen $$ *106 George Street, The Rocks, tel: 02 9251-2466.* This restaurant is interestingly set in a former sailors' home. For top views, ask for a table on the balcony.

The Wharf $$ *Pier 4, Hickson Road, Walsh Bay, tel: 02 9250-1761.* Not far from the Harbour Bridge, Pier 4 is known for its arts and theatre. Fine harbour views, good modern Australian cooking, fashionable/artsy clientele.

CITY CENTRE

Bistro-Fax $$ *27 O'Connell Street, tel: 02 8214 0400.* In the heart of the city, and part of the Radisson Hotel, this restaurant is true to the French bistro tradition of simple food served well, such as char-grilled beef fillet with field mushrooms, and grilled snapper.

Encasa $–$$ *423 Pitt Street, tel: 02 9211-4257.* Popular Spanish restaurant with very good tapas and seafood dishes. The paella is the real thing and takes 45 minutes to prepare.

Hyde Park Barracks Café $–$$ *Queens Square, Macquarie Street, tel: 02 9223-1815.* Sydney restaurant locations don't come more historic than this former convict barracks. Prisoners survived on porridge, bread and water; lunch these days is vastly more tempting. Breakfast and lunch only.

Marigold Citymark $–$$ *Levels 4 and 5, 683 George Street, Haymarket, tel: 02 9281-3388.* One of Sydney's most popular Chinese (Cantonese) restaurants, particularly liked for its *yum cha*. Service can be patchy.

MoS Café $–$$ *37 Phillip Street, tel: 02 9241-3636.* Located under the entrance to the Museum of Sydney, this café-restaurant is open for breakfast and lunch daily, and dinner Mon–Fri. Good-quality café cuisine, such as grilled ocean trout and various pasta dishes.

Post Seafood Brasserie $$ *1 Martin Place, tel: 02 9229-7744.* Modern Australian fare, with seafood dominating the menu. Located in the palatial former General Post Office building.

Tetsuya's $$$ *529 Kent Street, tel: 02 9267-2900, www.tetsuyas. com.* Probably the finest restaurant in Sydney, and perhaps one of the finest in the world. Fabulous flavours and masterful Japanese/ French combinations distinguish this acclaimed gourmet favourite. Reservations are essential, but you'll have to book months in advance.

DARLING HARBOUR

Chinta Ria Temple of Love $–$$ *Roof Terrace, Level 2, Cockle Bay Wharf, tel: 02 9264-3211.* Enjoy Malaysian food from an extensive menu, both old favourites *(nasi goreng, gado gado)* and new dishes like fish cooked in tamarind sauce with tomatoes and pineapple.

James Squire Brewhouse $ *22 The Promenade, King Street Wharf, tel: 02 8270-7999.* This microbrewery-cum-restaurant serves good, reliable pub grub, including fish 'n' chips, and steaks of all kinds. The beers are award-winning.

The Malaya $ *39 Lime Street, King Street Wharf, tel: 02 9279-1170.* Located near Darling Harbour, this Sydney institution serves up very good Malaysian fare.

Wagamama Noodle Bar $ *Lime Street, King Street Wharf, tel: 02 9299-6944.* Part of the worldwide Wagamama chain. Enjoy satisfying and inexpensive Japanese-influenced food seated at communal tables in a buzzy atmosphere.

EASTERN SUBURBS

Aki's $$ *Shop 1, The Wharf, 6 Cowper Wharf Road, Woolloomooloo, tel: 02 9332-4600.* One of the best Indian restaurants in the city. Located at the Woolloomooloo Bay Finger Wharf. Try for a table outside on the wharf for the harbour views.

Bayswater Brasserie $$ *32 Bayswater Road, Kings Cross, tel: 02 9357-2177.* Stylish restaurant in the heart of Kings Cross. The clientele is often intriguing, and so is the modern Australian cuisine.

Bill's $–$$ *433 Liverpool Street, Darlinghurst, tel: 02 9360-9631.* Renowned café-restaurant serving great-value breakfasts, lunches and dinners. Signature dishes include ricotta hotcakes with honeycomb butter. Very busy on weekends.

Billy Kwong $$ *3/355 Crown Street, Surry Hills, tel: 02 9332-3300.* Delicious Chinese food with a modern Australian twist in this tiny place. No reservations, so be prepared to wait, or arrive early.

Claude's $$$ *10 Oxford Street, Woollahra, tel: 02 9331-2325.* Malaysian-Chinese chef Chui Lee Luk puts a modern spin on classic French cuisine at one of Sydney's finest restaurants. Leave room for the delicious desserts. Three-course menu: A$135.

Erciyes $–$$ *409 Cleveland Street, Surry Hills, tel: 02 9319-1309.* Cheap, cheerful, and well-patronised Turkish restaurant specialising in *pide* (Turkish pizza). Bellydancers perform most Friday and Saturday nights. Cash preferred; credit-card identification necessary for cheques over A$60.

Longrain $$ *85 Commonwealth Street, Surry Hills, tel: 02 9280-2888.* A fashionable crowd flocks to this restaurant in an old warehouse, a 5-minute walk from Museum railway station, for the superb modern Thai cuisine. Dishes include snapper in a red curry sauce and caramelised pork hock. Communal tables. No reservations for dinner, so get there early (6pm) if you don't like waiting for a seat.

Mohr Fish $$ *202 Devonshire Street, Surry Hills, tel: 02 9318-1326.* An enticing variety of fresh fish and accompaniments. No reservations, but you can wait in the Shakespeare pub next door until a table clears. No credit cards.

Nepalese Kitchen $ *481 Crown Street, Surry Hills, tel: 02 9319-4264.* Cheap, spicy and delicious food from an uncommon cuisine.

Oh! Calcutta! $ *251 Victoria Street, Darlinghurst, tel: 02 9360-3650.* The emphasis is on modern Indian food, but the menu includes dishes from Pakistan and Afghanistan as well. Stir-fried kangaroo with sesame seeds is also on the menu.

Spice I Am $–$$ *90 Wentworth Avenue, Surry Hills, tel: 02 9280-0928.* Authentic Thai food served at high speed, in a bustling setting; takeaways also available. Great value for money. No reservations.

INNER WEST

Badde Manors Café $ *37 Glebe Point Road, Glebe, tel: 02 9660-3797.* Good vegetarian food for breakfast, lunch and dinner at this long-established café.

Darbar $ *134 Glebe Point Road, tel: 02 9660-5666.* Excellent southern Indian food in a capacious old sandstone building on Glebe's main dining and shopping street.

Fifi's $ *158 Enmore Road, Enmore, tel: 02 9550-4465.* Very fresh ingredients are used in this above-average and popular Lebanese restaurant, a few minutes further west of Newtown's bright lights.

La Disfida $ *109 Ramsay Street, Haberfield, tel: 02 9798-8299.* This place makes what many people regard as the best pizzas in Sydney, with thin bases cooked in a wood-fired oven. Also some pasta dishes. There's another good pizzeria around the corner at 73 Dalhousie Street, Napoli in Bocca.

Oscillate Wildly $$ *275 Australia Street, Newtown, tel: 02 9517-4700.* Just off Newtown's noisy main drag, this restaurant dishes up Modern Australian cuisine with the emphasis on meat, including kangaroo and rabbit. The desserts are wonderful. The restaurant's name comes from a song by the The Smiths, in praise of Oscar Wilde. Reservations essential.

Than Binh $ *11 King Street, Newtown, tel: 02 9557-1175.* Choose from the long menu or the daily specials blackboard at this Vietnamese eatery. As well as noodles, there are more substantial dishes such as twice-cooked duck leg. Very good vegetarian selection.

THE BEACHES

BONDI

Barzura $ *62 Carr Street, Coogee, tel: 02 9665-5546.* Modern Australian cooking, with influences ranging from Greek to Cajun. The appealing view across Coogee Beach adds extra sparkle.

Pompei's $–$$ *126–130 Roscoe Street, Bondi Beach, tel: 02 9365-1233.* A very popular and excellent corner eatery serving pizzas, home-made pasta and gelato. A cut above most Italian restaurants in this price range.

Sean's Panorama $$$ *270 Campbell Parade, Bondi Beach, tel: 02 9365-4924.* Always busy, and no wonder. Great modern Australian food served with verve within sight of Bondi's surf. You won't leave hungry. No credit cards.

MANLY

Out of Africa $$ *43–45 East Esplanade, Manly, tel: 02 9977-0055.* Moroccan restaurant near Manly wharf. Watch out for weekly specials that feature unusual meats such as ostrich and venison.

WATSONS BAY

Doyle's on the Beach $$–$$$ *11 Marine Parade, tel: 02 9337-2007.* Founded in 1885, Doyle's has the best location for alfresco dining in Sydney. The seafood here is fresh and simple, although the prices are on the high side; the beachfront views are dazzling, so bring your sunglasses. Visa, Mastercard only. A cheaper alternative is the excellent takeaway fish-and-chippery nearby, on Watsons Bay ferry wharf, opposite the park.

cultural diversity, world-class cuisine and spectacular architecture – with the easily accessible natural beauty of the surrounding harbour, beaches and green bushland. Moreover, Sydney's climate is pleasant and temperate for most of the year, seldom falling below 10°C (50°F) during the day in winter, with an average summer maximum of about 25°C (77°F).

Diverse Cityscape

Sydney Harbour, officially called Port Jackson, divides the city into north and south, with the great grey Harbour Bridge (completed in 1932) spanning the divide. Directly south of the bridge is Sydney's Central Business District (CBD), around which many of the city's key attractions – the Opera House, the historic Rocks district, Darling Harbour – are clustered. This area also hosts some of Sydney's most acclaimed restaurants, best shopping malls and premier arts venues.

Also to the south of the harbour, the eastern districts of Kings Cross and Paddington range from sleazy to gentrified and offer the best nightlife in the city. The beaches to the east of here include the famous Bondi. To the west, Chinatown and the Italian quarter of Leichhardt offer cheap eats, and further west still are the suburbs where most of Sydney's inhabitants live.

The landscapes north of the bridge are leafy, suburban and affluent, offering excellent views of the city and lovely beaches, from Manly on the edge of the harbour up to Palm Beach, about 40km (25 miles) from the CBD.

Harbour views

Melbourne people sometimes accuse Sydneysiders of being hedonistic anti-intellectuals obsessed with buying houses with harbour views. As the Melbourne-born playwright David Williamson put it in his play *Emerald City*: 'People in Sydney never waste time discussing the meaning of life – it's about getting yourself a water frontage.'